An important work in the new social history, Mr. Monkkonen's research modifies theories that the city drives its inhabitants into deviance and that status and stability inhered in the skilled occupations. He also lends clarity to the views about what kinds of criminal incidents represent pre-political rebellion.

Mr. Monkkonen received his doctorate from the University of Minnesota. He now teaches history at the University of North Carolina, Charlotte.

The Dangerous Class

The Dangerous Class

Crime and Poverty
in Columbus, Ohio, 1860-1885

Eric H. Monkkonen

Harvard University Press
Cambridge, Massachusetts
and London, England
1975

Library of Congress Cataloging in Publication Data

Monkkonen, Eric H 1942-

The Dangerous Class: Crime and Poverty in Columbus, Ohio, 1860-1885.

Includes index.

1. Crime and criminals—Columbus, Ohio—History. 2. Columbus, Ohio—Poor—History. 3. Columbus, Ohio—Social conditions. I. Title.

HV6795.C7M65   364′.9771′57   75-8917

ISBN 0-674-19058-0

Acknowledgments

There are many people and institutions to whom I owe a heavy debt of gratitude for this project. The staff of the Ohio Historical Society, especially Pat Gatherum, and the Franklin County Courthouse staff helped me find the basic materials and provided the needed microfilms. My advisers, George D. Green and John Modell, provided many hours of help, criticism, and encouragement. The Social Science Research Facilities Center provided keypunching and much computing assistance. Phillip Voxland, Jon Gross, Jim Young, Jerry Lutgen, provided specific aid and instruction, and Edwin Coover gave a fellow historian sympathy. My three research assistants, Shawne FitzGerald, Cheryl O'Brien and Kathleen Fitzgerald, did their tedious chores carefully and thoughtfully. Sue Cave and Diane Cloninger gave faithful typing. Jon Butler and Ray Michaelowski served me with helpful readings.

The material in this project was prepared under Grant No. 72 NI 99 1067 from the Manpower Development Assistance Division, Office of Criminal Justice Assistance, Law Enforcement Assistance Administration, U.S. Department of Justice. Researchers undertaking such projects under government sponsorship are encouraged to express freely their professional judgment. Therefore, points of view or opinions stated in this document do not necessarily represent the official position or policy of the U.S. Department of Justice.

The University of Minnesota Computing Center gave me the large computer time grant necessary for the computing. My wife provided moral and financial support. There are many more people to whom I am thankful: they know who they are and that my appreciation is real.

Contents

Tables

Figures

Factor maps of Ohio

The Dangerous Class

1 • Introduction

I do not complain that men of wealth expend their means as they prefer, but it seems not captious that I should wish crime and pauperism were as rare as the exhumed [bronze] treasures, that they might arouse equal zeal for deep research. There is, perhaps, yet hope, for these subjects have a claim to far greater antiquity inasmuch as they reach back to time immemorial, which assuredly antedates the bronzes.

Robert L. Dugdale (1877)

This study began by questioning a bit of conventional wisdom, almost a cliché: did urbanization and concurrent industrialization cause poverty and crime? The answer to this question, like the answers to so many simple questions, does not come easily, and a rather tortuous route must be taken to achieve qualified and complex answers. The question is important and should be dealt with, no matter how difficult, for to continue to assume that there has been a simple causal relationship between urbanization and crime and poverty does an intellectual injustice to cities, paupers, and criminals. Further, to find the roots of crime and poverty in the very nature of urban life needlessly indicts cities and clouds any deeper understanding of these social problems. If the generalizations so often made concerning nineteenth century cities and the criminals and paupers therein have any universality, the answers should be found in any growing industrial city, whether in New York in the early nineteenth century or in Columbus a little later. So Columbus, Ohio, between 1860 and 1885 is the specific case to which a general question is addressed, and although it is necessary to learn much of crime and poverty in Columbus, it must be remembered that the answers should be applicable to any city and its immediate hinterland in a similar stage of development.

The two most central social processes in nineteenth century American history are urbanization and industrialization. This book explores the impact of these two interacting processes on two groups of "anonymous Americans"—criminals and paupers. Far too little is known by historians about the bottom level of American society, and much of this book will examine, quantitatively, those persons who formed what was known as the dangerous class. Thus, this study is an exercise in history from the bottom up. It is a history of the process of urbanization and industrialization as it affected the lives of the poorer elements of society.

One of the least understood aspects of crime is its historical development. This is surprising in light of the assumptions we make about the nature, origins, and causes of crime. It is commonly assumed that contemporary urban industrial society has had to deal with unprecedented criminal problems, and more broadly, that vast social change has always produced those dropouts who constitute the poor and criminal classes. But historians have rarely studied the criminal experience to test these oft repeated assertions. Nor, despite our modern war on poverty, have we had many historical studies of the poor themselves. And of the scant studies of the poor, the criminal, or the police, almost every one is about New York, Boston, or Philadelphia, with New York being the most studied. The poor or criminal of the middle-sized American cities, where most of the urban population dwelt and where much of the impact of urbanization was felt, have been ignored.

Even though historians studying crime or the police have not done much hypothesis testing, they have clearly demonstrated one thing—that modern systems of social control, especially the police force, came about during the nineteenth century change from rural to urban society.[1] But no one has actually studied the criminal in the United States as Chevalier has done for Paris.[2]

Columbus, in Franklin County, Ohio, has several advantages for this kind of study. The city and its county changed from a traditional agricultural, commercial, and governmental center to a large, modern, and industrial city during the period 1860-85. Its middle range size and moderate growth rate are not unique, as those of New York or Chicago may well be. Further, its geographical position—in a rich agricultural hinterland, central to transportation, and near coal fields—is such that agricultural/industrial differences are measurable and industrial development was not purely dependent on resource exploitation. But the major advantage in studying Columbus is that its industrial development came relatively late, after 1870.[3] This meant that the city had forty years to develop as a commercial, agricultural, and political service center—time in which to develop a social structure based on a nonindustrial economic base, a structure which should show clearly the effects of industrial change.

Columbus's late industrial growth has another very practical benefit for those who would study its inhabitants—the records are still available. The Criminal Court of Franklin County has always been a part of the Common Pleas Court and still is: but since 1860 its records have been kept separately. And for the period under study, 1860-85, there is a consistent set of records, generated by one court, of indictable offenses—an unfortunately rare situation for this period. Of additional importance, the records of the county poorhouse (officially called the County Infirmary), which list paupers by name and age, have also been preserved from 1867 on. Other, supplementary sources for this county also exist—the manuscript United States censuses and city directories—both of which are informative about those people who came to be the paupers and criminals of Franklin County. And, finally, enough economic data are available to make some inferences about the economic structure of Columbus and its hinterland. It is, in other words, the ideal place for a case study.

This study, for the most part, is quantitative, with three levels of analysis. The first employs traditional aggregate methods and multivariate statistics. Using published state statistics, I have created urban/rural crime indexes, by type of crime, comparing all urban areas in the state with Columbus and with rural areas. These indexes are used to measure change over time for urban places, for Columbus specifically, and for the state as a whole. The results are used to analyze change in aggregate criminal patterns based on economic, agricultural, and socioeconomic data. Chapter 2, therefore, provides a context for the more concentrated analysis which follows.

The second level of analysis is also based on aggregate statistics, but those specifically relating to Columbus and its county. These statistics are derived from the unpublished county court and poorhouse records, rather than the published secretary of state's reports. There are three main reasons to analyze carefully these unpublished records. First, there was a time lag of up to a year between the first recording of a crime by the county clerk and its subsequent publication by the secretary of state.

Second, only a small amount of the total was published. In the case of the poorhouse records, the state merely published the number of inhabitants in residence at a given moment, completely neglecting the turnover during a year. Fewer than 20 percent of the total crimes were ever published, mainly because few ever actually came to trial. Third, and most important, more information is available about individuals in the unpublished county records. For the criminals, only one individual characteristic is available, sex, but this is significant. The poorhouse records, on the other hand, are loaded with information on individuals from age and place of birth to such personal descriptions as "destitute" or "old hussy." Thus, from the descriptive statistics on these two sets of records, we can get a much closer look at the criminals and paupers of Columbus and its hinterland than the state records can ever provide.

The third level of analysis deals with these individuals. It uses the names of criminal defendants and paupers admitted to the poorhouse, emphasizing the linkage of these lists with the city directories and the 1870 manuscript census. This linking is important, for through it the aggregative conclusions of Chapter 2 are tested and improved on the basis of knowledge about individual criminals and paupers. The questions of social origins and socioeconomic status, of changing occupational structure, of ethnicity, age, and family are all examined. The completeness of these linkages shows the relationship of the criminals to the paupers and establishes the degree of their representation in the census and city directories.

The book concludes with an analysis of the dangerous class, a nineteenth century concept that includes five different groups of people—rural criminals, urban criminals, rural paupers, urban paupers, and tramps. In Columbus, at least, this dangerous class is found to blend with the normal population, showing more differences of degree than kind. Over one fourth of the county population had no property so that distinctions between the bottom fourth of society and the paupers are rather hazy, to say the least.

There were important changes in the microstructure of crime and poverty, but the overall incidence relative to the population stayed remarkably stable over the period investigated. The central hypothesis with which this study began asserted that rural/urban migrations and the change from the nonindustrial city to the industrial city created both a pauper and a criminal class. It was predicted that these classes had emerged as specific occupational and ethnic groups failed to adapt to the shift from traditional to industrial society and became urban criminals and paupers. This hypothesis is disproved, or at least it is not confirmed. There is little or no evidence that urban growth or industrial growth affected the crime rates or poverty rates of Columbus. This should make us suspicious about contemporary observations of the effects of urban life on crime and poverty, for if nineteenth century origins mean anything, the relationship was subtle and complex.

The second hypothesis tested in this study, that poverty caused by employment shifts due to industrialization led to crime, is also unconfirmed. Criminals were found to be quite different from paupers—of higher status—and, if anything, crime led to poverty more than poverty led to crime. Paupers and tramps, on the very bottom of society, were apparently too oppressed to resort to theft or other criminal activity.

Finally, the reader must be forewarned: this study has many numbers in it. There are some statistics, especially in Chapter 2, many graphs, and many tables. It is my conviction that one must use numbers to study the past when the object of study is a large group of people: anything else ignores many for few. The use of numbers and statistics allows the past to be personalized in a most important way, for the behavior of all counts and is counted. And although some of the biases of the past come with the numbers, many of the sins of historians can be corrected—the ignoring of women, ethnic and racial differences, and the overemphasis on elites and elite sources.

2 • An Ecological Analysis of Ohio, 1867-1883

It is doubtless the fact that offences due to idleness, to poverty, and to weak wills are oftener found in the cities than in the country.
   Fred G. Pettigrove (1892)

Although the criminals and paupers of Franklin County are the ultimate subjects of this study, we must begin with the whole state of Ohio. There are several reasons why: first, some sort of check is needed to make sure that Columbus and Franklin County did not exhibit special characteristics which made them unique in the context of the state. Second, by looking at broader statewide patterns, hypotheses can be made and tested to help in guiding the deeper, more microcosmic analysis. And third, by following this statewide examination with a look at one county and its large city one can discover whether or not it is methodologically feasible to make inferences about individuals from the rather poor quality published data available for Ohio, and incidentally, for many other states as well. Should this prove possible, there is hope for more state level research in crime and poverty without resorting to digging in local records.

The concern, then, is in causally explaining crime, and to a lesser extent, poverty, in relation to the urban/industrial setting of the state of Ohio in the late nineteenth century. As an ecological analysis, the focus here is on the relationship between social behavior and its environment, defined in measurable terms. For example, was rape an urban phenomenon or did it become one? One way to ask this question is to simply correlate rape rates with urbanization rates. But to pose a question in this manner is to imply an important caveat: there may be an unknown outside influence for which we have not accounted and therefore not measured. For instance, continuing with the same example, had we discovered the incidence of rape to be much higher in cities, we would probably infer that urban life styles had something to do with the reasons men rape women. But we could easily have overlooked an unmeasurable possibility—perhaps rural men came to the cities in order to rape and then retreated to the country. Thus, here, as in any ecological analysis, we must keep our logic under scrutiny. Much of this chapter deals with the problems of quantitatively defining urbanism and industrialism. Since the urban/industrial environment as well as crime and poverty are of interest to historians, it is hoped that this aspect of the study will contribute to our understanding both of urban/industrial growth and of crime and poverty. In addition, there may well be a specifiable relationship between measurable social behavior, such as crime, and the structure of the larger society—a relationship which, if understood, allows the measured behavior to stand as an indicator of change in the society. Crime can be a window on social change and structure. Thus, by deepening our understanding of crime and poverty, we may be able to make one step toward a larger goal—the quantifiable measure of an otherwise unmeasurable phenomenon, social change. While this study does not purport to establish the relationship of crime and poverty to the environment specifically enough to create indices of social change, it should be seen as a step in that direction.

Chapter 2 is organized into sections as follows. In the first section the argument relating crime and poverty to urbanization is presented and the general characteristics of Ohio are discussed. In the second section historical data are used to develop a measure of relative urbanization; this is a rather technical section which involves the use of factor analysis. The third section discusses the complexities of published crime statistics and simplifies the categories by grouping all offenses into eight types of criminal activity. In the fourth section the measures of crime, pauperism, urbanization, and industrialization are all brought together and compared. And the fifth section summarizes and expands upon the whole business.

Crime and Urbanization

Because in this chapter I have decided to look at crime and not the criminal, pauperism and not the pauper, I have committed myself to a definition of crime and poverty as systematic social phenomena. That is, I view crime and economic dependency as the rational behavior of individuals selecting from available alternative modes of behavior, rather than as aberrant behavior. Certainly many nineteenth century spokesmen (and twentieth century as well) would tell us instead to look at the actors themselves for character flaws and moral evils. For this analysis, I reject an explanation of crime and poverty which limits itself to individual abberations; after all, a criminal offense is a formally recognized social event, an interaction between the legal system of the state and the individual offender. To study the actor in order to affix blame, an emotion-laden word for cause, simply misses the whole point of trying to explain crime. For the historian especially, the ultimate reason in studying crime is to understand the whole society, and focusing only on the individual leads to a misperception both of the society and of crime.

Instead, I view the criminal or economically dependent person as making sensible choices governed by the alternatives within his specific situation. This view is a necessary assumption for an ecological analysis which rests on the postulate of a predictable and therefore rational set of relationships. Otherwise, if we think that the causal origins of crime and pauperism are to be found within the individual and not in the environment, then an ecological analysis is irrelevant.

Adna F. Weber, one of the United States' first statistically oriented students of urbanization, admitted in 1889 that "criminal statistics undoubtedly put the cities in a bad light."[1] Weber's admission should not surprise us, however, for throughout the nineteenth century and down to the present, cities have been characterized as the breeding places of criminals and paupers. Finley Peter Dunne's Mr. Dooley, in trying to "tell what makes wan man a thief an' another man a saint," allows that "Sometimes I think they'se poison in the life iv a big city. Th' flowers won't grow here no more thin they wud in a tannery, an' th' bur-rds have no song; an' th' childer iv dacint men an' women come up hard in th' mouth an' with their hands raised again their kind."[2]

In 1872, writing of his work among the "dangerous classes" in New York, Charles Loring Brace, implicitly blamed the city for the creation and maintenance of the dangerous class. Although he was greatly concerned with intervening variables, like alcohol, overcrowding, and bad marriage ties, one of his favorite cures for young paupers and criminals was transplanting them to a farm and letting its healing virtues regenerate them. In one curious passage, Brace finds the effects of constant moving about within cities to be the negation of the effects of heredity, presumably of either bad genes or good genes. Thus, although the good forces of family life—"that continuity of influence"—may be destroyed, geographic mobility also destroys forces of evil. "The mill of American life," claimed Brace, "which grinds up so many delicate and fragile things, has its uses, when it is turned on the vicious fragments of the lower strata of society."[3]

While less analytic than Brace or Weber or even Mr. Dooley, and more concerned with the intervening variables than with the city itself, Robert Hunter, who published his classic, *Poverty*, in 1904, also implicitly found the city to be the breeding place for criminals and paupers. "The city child," he claimed, "becomes criminal because it can almost be said that in these districts the only thing to do worthy of a boy's spirit are those things which are against the law."[4] Writing twenty years later than Charles Loring Brace, Hunter could see the impossibility of the farm cure for the dangerous class of the city, and he concentrated on specific urban evils like overcrowding and disease.

Nevertheless, the tradition, at least as old as Jefferson's characterization of cities as "sores upon the body politic," which finds cities as the causal element in the creation of a dangerous class has remained with us through the present. Urbanization continues to be the major ecological explanation of the social ills of crime and poverty, and few dispute it.[5] Marshall B. Clinard's classic article, "The Process of Urbanization and Criminal Behavior," which appeared in 1942, set the tone for many subsequent criminological studies.[6] He found that the socially disorganizing effects of urbanization caused crime, for even offenders from rural backgrounds had urban lifestyles and social backgrounds. Now, more than thirty years after the appearance of Clinard's article, cities are synonymous with crime and poverty for most people. We read FBI crime statistics to see which of the top 25 cities has become the most dangerous in which to live, and many Americans move to rural places in an effort to find freedom from the fear posed by the dangerous class.

Concern with urbanization and crime continues to rank high in the contemporary study of criminology. Marshall B. Clinard's popular text, *The Sociology of Deviant Behavior*, devotes a whole chapter to urbanization and crime. "The spread of urbanization," asserts Clinard, "has almost everywhere—whether in the United States, Europe, Latin America, Africa, or Asia—been accompanied by a marked increase in various forms of deviant behavior."[7] Using evidence running from Emile Durkheim's classic work to recent FBI crime statistics, which show two to twenty times as high incidence rates for urban as compared to rural crime, Clinard establishes the contemporary problem of urban crime. Then, citing his own study of crime in developing nations, he creates a developmental model of cities and crime to establish the causal link between urbanization as a process and the resulting increase in deviant behavior. Thus, students of criminology continue with the view that urban life creates criminality, even though no one any more suggests, with Charles Loring Brace, a rural solution to criminal behavior.

Clearly, the best place to begin an ecological analysis of crime and poverty in the nineteenth century is with the most dominant and respected modern hypothesis. Specifically, our hypothesis is that crime and poverty will be more prevalent in those areas of Ohio which we define as urban. From this rather large hypothesis, we can make some more explicit hypotheses concerning specific kinds of crime.

We must assume that industrial society, as opposed to traditional society, develops ways for strangers to deal with one another. This happens not only because industrial societies have large numbers of anonymous people, but because of the need for large industrial systems to depend on the interchangeability of persons as well as parts. Industrial society has more secondary relationships (that is, people will be known to one another in one role only: for example, workmate or neighbor, but not both) than traditional society. Identifying another person's role is more difficult, simply because of numbers of people and the perceptual nature of secondary relationships. As a result, strangers will not be discriminated against as in a society where strangers are outsiders. Pluralism is a necessary fact of urban and industrial life, not by anyone's choice, but by necesssity. Both because of the increased size and scale of urban and industrial society and because of the urban area's function as a social service center, all opportunities are increased and made more visible.

On the basis of these assumptions we can devise several testable hypotheses. First, because of its plural cultural groups and because of its nature as a service center, a modern urban society will decrease the prosecution of those crimes which are moral offenses to some, cultural characteristics for others, and occupations for others. Thus, such crimes as gambling or prostitution or drinking will increase in incidence but decrease in prosecution. However, the possibility for a special case remains: the city which rationalizes such crimes as a part of its economic service function. In this case, prosecution would increase, as a recent study of an unnamed midwestern town which became a vice center during the early twentieth century shows: mild prosecution increased, functioning as a tax.[8] Unless Columbus fit the special situation and was a vice center as well as a political center, we can predict that its incidence of moral offenses remained stable as it industrialized and grew.

Second, because of the numerical size and decreasing physical proximity of different classes in modern urban society, the increasingly visible differences between the poor and the rich coupled with the decreasing chance of their personal acquaintance will increase both the incidence of theft and its prosecution. Need, a constant, should have been augmented by opportunity, with the restraint of personal involvement and responsibility gone. This potential has been implicitly recognized by society's ranking of the seriousness of most direct forms of theft, robbery especially, as being more serious than anonymous and less direct theft: a person who takes directly from another is considered far more dangerous than someone who shoplifts, and the shoplifter is viewed as being more threatening than someone who merely fails to return lost goods. We expect anonymity and opportunity to lift the restraints against theft: thus urban growth should have fostered an increase in theft. Third, the possibility for anonymity in modern urban life, coupled with the need for secure monetary transactions with strangers, will increase both the incidence and prosecution of crimes against property by trick and deception.

Recent studies emphasize that violent crimes against persons tend to occur within a circle of friends and relatives, while rape is most often committed against casual acquaintances.[9] Therefore, if we assume with the classical sociologists that urban life is characterized by secondary relationships and casual acquaintances, crimes of personal

11

violence, except for rape, should have decreased as urbanization increased. Rape should have increased.

Finally, we might expect the incidence of pauperism to increase as the city grew. This prediction is made upon the observations of both nineteenth century observers and contemporary theorists that urban life fosters pauperism and dependence.[10] The reasons for the causal relationship of poverty and the city have not been made entirely clear, but it has something to do with the myth of the country life as being stable, simple, and open—where hard work is rewarded and honesty abounds. As Brace observed when explaining his farm cure for the dangerous class, "The cultivators of the soil are in America our most solid and intelligent class."[11] Deviance, we can conclude, should not only have variously increased or decreased in nineteenth century cities, but its nature should have changed.

Ohio in the late nineteenth century has all the requisites for a case study of crime and poverty. Although its proportion of the total United States population was declining slightly, both in 1870 and 1880 it stayed the third most populous of the states. While large-scale farming was declining somewhat compared to the rest of the nation, in 1880 the total number of farms was second in the country. And at the same time, manufacturing, measured in terms of male hands employed, ranked Ohio fourth among the states, as did total manufacturing capitalization.[12]

More important than Ohio's position relative to other states, however, was the internal change taking place. As shown in Table 1, this change is best reflected in its increasing share of the dollar added value of manufacturing both per capita and per factory hand, as well as by its increasing share of the total national manufacturing output—from 6.5 to 6.7 percent. The state's increasing industrialization is responsible for both the decline in importance of large farming and the increase in small farms, with small farms serving both as truck farms and as an upward escape route for some from urban industrial employment.[13]

This economic change in the state did not go unnoticed, even in smaller towns. Sherwood Anderson writes of his hometown of Clyde in this period: "There was something strange happening to our town that must have been happening at about the same time to thousands of American towns: a sudden and almost universal turning of men from

Table 1.   Industrial growth measured by value added by manufacturing, per capita, for Franklin County, Ohio, and the United States, 1860-1890

| | | | | Ratio | |
| | | | | County: | County: |
Year	U.S.	Ohio	Franklin County	U.S.	Ohio
1860	$27.10	$22.18	$28.51	1.05	1.28
1870	45.23	42.24	42.30	.94	1.00
1880	39.33	41.58	61.38	1.56	1.48
1890	36.40	81.87	96.57	2.65	1.18

Source: Computed from the *Manufacturing* volumes of the 8th-11th U.S. Census.

the old handicrafts toward our modern life of the machines . . . It was kind of a fever, an excitement in the veins of the people."[14] In Cincinnati, which was no longer called the "Queen City of the West," the process of suburbanization had been carried far enough that the wealthy no longer lived in the city center; twentieth century land use patterns had been established.[15] Ohio was not a frontier anymore: the West had become the Midwest. If crime and poverty, or typical configurations of crime and poverty, were causally connected with the development of the modern industrial city, this is the period when such patterns should have emerged in Ohio.

The Development of a Multivariate Measure of Urbanization

Before examining the relationship of urban industrial development to crime and poverty, the concepts of urban and industrial must be measurable, a task less simple than appearances suggest. One would expect that either population density or the proportion of persons living in towns over 2,500 would serve as a measure of a county's degree of urbanization. Table 2 demonstrates the difficulty of this approach.

Two of the ten most dense counties in Ohio in 1870, Stark and Mahoning, and two of the ten highest per capita urban counties, Crawford and Butler, appear in one list only. In other words, two apparently similar ways of measuring the urban counties give some-

Table 2.   *Rank order of the ten most dense and highest per capita urban counties, 1870, by county*

County	Density[a]	County	Per capita urban
Hamilton	756.9	Hamilton	.831
Cuyahoga	431.9	Cuyahoga	.813
Lucas	196.4	Lucas	.747
Montgomery	168.9	Franklin	.595
Franklin	161.3	Clarke	.494
Erie	123.7	Montgomery	.492
Stark[b]	110.4	Erie	.485
Summit	106.0	Crawford[b]	.403
Clarke	104.3	Butler[b]	.391
Mahoning[b]	102.3	Summit	.377

Source: Calculated from 1870 U.S. Census and from the 16th U.S. Census (1940), *Measurement of Geographic Area* by Malcolm J. Proudfoot.

[a] In persons per square mile.

[b] These counties did not rank in the first ten of the other set of rankings.

what different results. Which is the seventh most urban county, Erie with the city of Sandusky, or Stark with the city of Canton? Or which is the fourth, Montgomery with the city of Dayton, or Franklin with Columbus?

To illustrate the subtle but important difference made by the way "urbanness" is measured, several crime rates and the pauperism rate for 1870 were correlated with both the density and per capita urban measures. The second part of Table 3 displays the differing results. A glance tells that in two cases, gambling violations and theft rates, there were large differences given by the two measures of urbanization. And there is no guide as to which is the better column to use for interpretation: the per capita urban column with its emphasis on murder and theft and a deemphasis of gambling, or the density column, with a sharp change in theft and increased emphasis on gambling.

Table 3.   Correlation (Pearson's R) between deviance rates and
two measures of urbanization

Category	Per Capita Urban[a]	Density	Difference
Pauperism	-.002	-.060	.048
Murder	.401	.329	.071
Rape	.017	-.030	.047
Assault and battery	-.192	-.167	.025
Theft	.254	.186	.068
Theft by trick	.001	.025	.026
Liquor violation	-.055	-.144	.089
Gambling	.022	.136	.114

[a]This is the number of people in towns over 2,500 divided by the total county population.

Both sets of data in Table 2 and Table 3 demonstrate the necessity of carefully deciding how the various counties are to be ranked as to their relative degrees of urbanization. The choice of measures can clearly determine the outcome of the investigation. Therefore, before performing any statistical comparisons of crime and pauper rates to urban and rural counties, industrial and farming counties, we must very carefully develop a measurement method. The remainder of this section will explain the creation of the urbanization and industrialization measures that are used through the rest of this chapter.

The first requirement of the problem is to devise multivariate measures that include as many of the subtle things which go to make up city as possible. These measures will be utilized to rank the individual county's "urbanness." Such a procedure is an advantage, for the concept of "urban" or "industrial" is quite complex, and multiple variables best capture this complexity. The data available in the U.S. census dictated the choice of variables utilized in this study, but within these limitations a sophisticated measure could be created. Twelve variables relating to social, economic, and geographic definitions of an urban area were selected. The variables define a city as a place with a heterogeneous, mobile, and dense population, where property values are high and there are few large farms, where manufacturers concentrate and there is a high proportion of workers, both adults and children.

Rather than arbitrarily combine the twelve variables which make up the measures of "urbanness," factor analysis was employed to order and rank all the variables. Essentially, factor analysis identifies similar patterns of covariation in large groups of variables, constructing "factors" which account for as much common variance as possible.[16] Thus, one of the major uses of factor analysis is to reduce the raw data on many variables and to combine the variables into a smaller set of artificial variables called variates. Here, for instance, it was possible to combine a dozen variables into two or three variates. Not only are these variates easier to understand when compared with the crime and pauperism rates, but they are each composed of only the correct proportions of the dozen original variables. Most important, these variates can be manipulated like real variables in further analysis. And rather than correlate a dozen variables with theft, for instance, just two or three variates may be brought in.

The object, then of the factor analysis was to create an urban factor that could be used to avoid the problem demonstrated in Table 2, that of measuring a county's degree of urbanization. This urban factor provides the basis for the urban variate. A precautionary note should be added. Because of the unfamiliar jargon, the subsequent discussion may be rather difficult to follow: to such readers my admonition is to try to get the substantive sense and not worry about the statistical logic. I have been forced by lack of data to exclude potentially relevant variables, such as age structure, in the factor analysis. Thus, the measure of "urban" employed below may be imperfect; but its strength is in its definitional precision and clear derivation from a rationally selected universe of variables.

Table 4 shows the results of the factor analysis; each number is called the factor "loading" and represents the contribution of each variable (at the left of the table) to the factor. Traditionally, only factor loadings above plus or minus .4 are considered important, and these have been underlined in the table.[17] The bottom row shows the amount of variation among all the variables for which a factor accounts, an indication of the factor's explanatory strength. The composition of the major factors reveals much about the urban structure of Ohio and deserves a close examination.

Factor 1 is obviously the best indicator of urbanization and industrialization, confirming the expectations that guided the selection of the relevant variables. It accounts for 54 percent of the common variation in the total set of variables in 1870. The structure of Factor 1 for 1870 is interesting both in itself and in comparison with Factor 1 for 1880. The variables for male manufacturing hands (per capita) and the dollar added value of manufacturing (per capita), rather than population density or the number of persons in towns over 2,500, prove to contribute the most to this factor, while the foreign born population (per capita) contributes almost as much as density. Just below the foreign born variable in loading comes persons under sixteen employed in manufacturing, followed by the urban dwellers variable and the number of women workers (per capita).

To summarize: Factor 1 for 1870 may be defined as an urban/industrial factor with three kinds of contributing variable—first, manufacturing, defined by dollar added value and male hands; second, urbanization, defined by foreign born and population density; and a third group of variables defining urbanization by political boundaries and those two groups of people who most often come to mind when we think of early urban manufacturing—women and child workers. And parenthetically, farm value and number of farms per capita load negatively on this factor, confirming our expectations.

Over the decade between 1870 and 1880, urban/rural differences had increased considerably, and this change is best reflected in the compositional change and strengthening of Factor 1, the urban factor. Its gain in explanatory power, accounting for 70 percent of the total variation, is almost 16 percent more than in 1870. This heightened urban-rural distinction captured by the factor analysis will be made even more apparent when the crime and pauperism rates are brought into the picture.

Factor 1 for 1880 is the straightforward and significant urban/industrial factor which had been predicted for both 1870 and 1880. This factor has three clusters of variables, the strongest consisting of male and young factory hands and the dollar added manufacturing value. The second cluster is the pair of variables which Table 2 showed to be in a difficult relationship, population density and the per capita population of towns with over 2,500 inhabitants. While not so tightly

Table 4. Factor loadings for 1870 and 1880

Variable	Urban/industrial factor	Hinterland factor	Manufacturing factor	Rural factor
1870				
Minorities[a]	-.05637	-.05405	-.05336	-.53256
Density	.77570	.03310	.14300	-.11914
Urban[a]	.62579	-.17384	.34245	-.16861
Foreign born[a]	.77463	.28947	-.04632	.10696
Small farms[a]	.22900	.93244	-.02181	-.04011
Manufacturing value[a]	.88424	-.05825	.00904	.17768
Male hands[a]	.87710	-.08731	-.01794	.16249
Child hands[a]	.72867	.20287	.49864	-.13105
Female hands[a]	.62473	.06007	.66075	-.01336
Farm value[a]	-.46103	-.17990	.54726	.27791
Property value[a]	.08176	.02617	.89931	.07152
Farms[a]	-.75483	.17333	.06774	.46212
Percentage of farms under 20 acres	-.27683	.93903	.02743	.19740
Percentage of variation accounted for by factor	54	21	18	7

Variable	Urban/industrial factor	Hinterland factor	Property factor
1880			
Minorities[a]	.03493	-.04714	.20802
Density	.84539	.00138	.09917
Urban[a]	.83385	-.12862	.19002
Foreign born[a]	.73108	.00999	-.11905
Small farms[a]	.75858	.51260	.15443
Manufacturing value[a]	.92041	-.00074	.11563
Male hands[a]	.89294	-.10466	-.04972
Child hands[a]	.87519	-.16049	-.00788
Female hands[a]	.77301	-.09738	.15169
Farm value[a]	-.61210	.29957	.42453
Property value[a]	.08324	.30199	1.05253
Farms[a]	-.80492	.27706	-.15409
Percentage of farms under 20 acres	-.22230	.99151	.03257
Percentage of variation accounted for by factor	70	21	8

[a] Per capita

related, the remaining three variables in this factor add a needed dimension to the definition of urban/industrial. Working women and foreign born fill out the manufacturing and population clusters, while the small farm variable suggests that between 1870 and 1880 the immediate hinterland of urban areas had become more specialized in filling urban agricultural needs.

The structure of the urban factor for 1880, unlike its counterpart for 1870, has more clear groupings of variables, indicating a maturing urban economy, with rational and contiguous locations of economic and social resources. Three manufacturing related variables cluster together with the highest factor loadings, while the two population related variables cluster right below them. The only apparent inconsistencies are with the women workers variable, falling below the urban population cluster near the small farm variable, which has gained greatly in importance since 1870.

Because of the shift in the composition of Factor 1 between 1870 and 1880, two slightly different operational measures of urban areas are employed in this book. The definition for 1870 emphasizes seven variables, while for 1880 another variable, the number of small farms per capita, is added, and a slightly different variable ordering is used for 1880. Both measures are of the same thing—urban/industrial areas—but that thing had changed over the decade, and there would be little sense in using the 1870 measure in 1880.

Although the hinterland factor, or Factor 2, appears to be the same in both 1870 and 1880, its changed loading values indicate a significant agricultural change. In both years it accounts for 21 percent of the common variance, and in both years its largest loadings are on the same two variables—the per capita small farms variable and the percentage of farms under twenty acres variable. In 1870 these two variables load evenly, but by 1880, the percent small farm variable loads .99 and the per capita small farm variable loads only .55. What has happened is that between 1870 and 1880 there was increasing geographical specialization in land use so that the more purely agricultural a county was, the less likely it was to have small marginal or truck farms. Thus, Factor 2, which at first glance appears to be simply an agricultural factor, is really a hinterland truck farming and marginal farm factor.

The technique of factor mapping can be used to confirm this interpretation. A factor map uses each county's factor score to present visually the geographical distribution of factors. The factor maps used here were shaded on those counties with strong positive factor scores and left unshaded on negative or zero score counties. The 1870 maps show clearly how Factor 2 incorporates both hinterland farming and marginal farm counties, two conceptually and spatially different entities. With the exception of Hamilton County (containing Cincinnati) in the extreme southwest corner of the state, most of the Factor 2 counties are adjacent to, but do not coincide with, the urban/industrial counties that are identified on the Factor 1 map. The six Factor 2 counties in the northwest corner of the map and the one on the eastern edge are the only counties that do not abut urban areas. These relatively isolated counties contained the poor, marginal farms, and although these farms had developed on a different basis than those in the urban hinterland ecosystem, their small acreage caused them to be included in Factor 2.

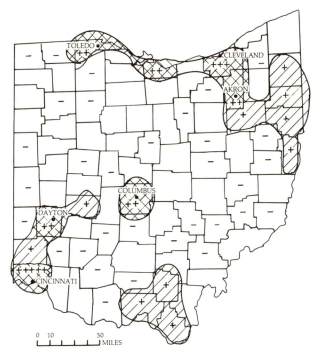

Factor 1. 1870, Urban/industrial

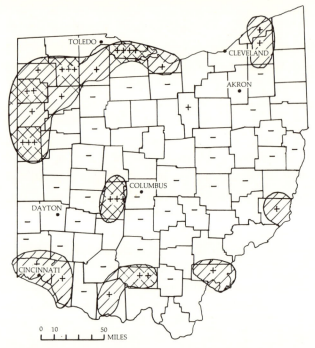

Factor 2. 1870, Hinterland/marginal farms

Factor 3. 1870, Agriculture

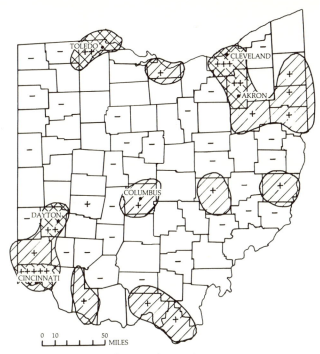

Factor 1. 1880, Urban/industrial

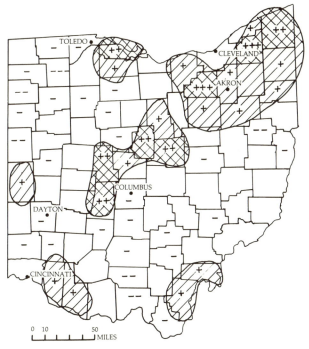

Factor 2. 1880, Hinterland

These marginal farms, true to their noncompetitive nature, had declined in importance by 1880 as the state's urban/industrial economy matured. As the Factor 2 map for 1880 demonstrates, all the counties strongly affected by this factor abut, surround, or, in a few cases, overlap the urban/industrial counties identified on the Factor 1 maps. Clearly, Ohio's improving transportation system and developing urban network had had a dramatic impact on agriculture over the decade, for the 1870 marginal farming counties in the northwest have negative scores by 1880.

All the factors discussed above will be important for the ensuing discussion of crime and pauperism. In converting the factors to variates, the relative statistical weighting of each county is taken into account so that each may be treated as a case, and its score (factor score coefficient) for the three variates may be compared to its crime and pauper rates. Rather than talk about number of farms per capita or child laborers per capita, we will be able to talk about the urban variate or the hinterland variate.

The Derivation of Crime Rates for Ohio in the Nineteenth Century

The crime rates for this study were derived from the *Annual Report* of the Secretary of State of Ohio. Instead of using the figures for the two single years of 1870 and 1880, two sets of three years each were averaged to gain greater stability and to allow the inclusion of those counties which failed to report occasionally. As the federal census data were taken for 1870 and 1880, the periods for the crime rates are labeled here by these dates for convenience, even though the *Reports* used were for 1867, 1868, 1870 and 1881, 1882, 1883 (1869 and 1880 were not published). Since the *Reports* list only those crimes brought to trial, the rates may lack the stability which a larger number would have provided.

In order to estimate the approximate percentage of all criminal cases which came to court but were unreported by the state, it is necessary to examine the data which I gathered separately for the Franklin County Courts. Unfortunately, the terminology used by the Secretary of State and the Court Clerk differs, and the state report even uses a category which includes "etc." Eleven and two tenths percent of all Franklin County cases were found guilty, 4.4 percent not guilty, 5.2

percent were "laid away," 15.5 percent were *nolle prossed*, 4.2 percent were dismissed with costs, 26.4 percent had no bill of indictment written, and 32.6 percent were simply dismissed without comment. The state, on the other hand, reported cases which were continued, acquittals, *nolle prosequi's* (and, in the same category, the "etc.'s"), and guilty's. My estimate, therefore, is that about one fourth of the Franklin County Court cases were reportable to the Secretary of State. Thus, although this study is not concerned with the absolute magnitude of crime on the state level, it should be kept in mind that the state data represents about 30 percent of the court activity: it is, in other words, a sample.

This creates two problems for the ensuing analysis. First, in many cases the low total number of offenses for a county have forced me to eliminate some categories from the overall analysis or combine them with other similar crime categories. Second, the probability that the official *Reports* may be hopelessly inaccurate must be acknowledged. I have proceeded on the assumption that the errors are randomly distributed. Of course, the only way to test such an assumption would be to regather the data reported to the Secretary of State, an immense task.

Table 5 shows the 45 different crime categories that appeared in the *Annual Report* of 1883 and the total number of prosecutions for the same year, to give some idea of the total numbers which are involved. These prosecutions are spread across 88 counties, and one can quickly see that for many categories, there simply were not enough offenses in the whole state to give any kind of distribution pattern. Further, it made no sense in this study to preserve legal distinctions that do not reflect useful social or theoretical distinctions. Therefore, these 45 different categories were collapsed into eight categories of similar crimes, which are shown on the right-hand side of Table 5. (There was some unavoidable information loss involved in this collapsing, about 18 percent, slightly more than the 16 percent loss for the county level aspect of this study.) And some interesting but difficult to classify categories, such as "malicious destruction of property," had to be dropped because of the small number of reported prosecutions and the lack of comparability to other categories.

The logic of the eight new crime categories in Table 5 should be

Table 5. *Crime categories and total number of prosecutions for Ohio in 1883*

Crime		Prosecutions ($N=6,325$)
Murder in the first degree		57
Murder in the second degree	Murder[a]	41
Manslaughter		33
Rape		40
Assault and battery		750
Robbery		101
Burglary		471
Grand larceny	Theft	373
Petit larceny		339
Horse stealing		109
Blackmail		9
Embezzlement		85
Receiving, buying or concealing stolen property	Theft by trick	45
Obtaining money or goods by false pretenses		128
Forgery		237
Offenses against gambling laws		122
Offenses against liquor laws		2,606
Riot		22
Breach of peace and all other offenses against public peace		136
Illegal voting and all other offenses against suffrage	All other statutory offenses	6
Perjury and subornation of perjury		45
Bribery and attempt to bribe, and all other offenses against public justice		48
All offenses against public health		9

continued

Crime		Prosecutions (N=6,325)
Bigamy		22
Incest		11
Adultery and fornication	All other	21
Seduction under promise of marriage	statutory	12
Keeping house of ill-fame	offenses	129
Indecent exposure, and all other offenses against chastity and morality		121

Unclassified	Prosecutions (N=1,167)
Administering poison with intent to kill	3
Attempt to procure abortion	12
Maiming or disfiguring another	13
Assault with intent to kill	466
Assault with intent to commit rape or robbery	56
Pointing firearms at any person	22
All other crimes against the person	109
Arson	45
Obstructing railroad track	7
Malicious destruction of property	61
Malicious destruction of trees and crops	16
All other crimes against property	154
Carrying concealed weapons	127
Prosecution for all offenses not named heretofore	69

Source: Annual Report, Secretary of State of Ohio, 1883.

[a] The classifications after the brackets are my own and in some places differ from convention. Robbery, for instance, I have judged significant for the theft involved, not for the personal violence. Many of the unclassified crimes are judged so because they do not clearly fit in any of the newly created categories—assault with intent to kill, for instance—or because one cannot be sure from the state reports what the exact nature of the offense was.

readily apparent. Four of the original categories had sufficiently many cases and distinct definitions that they could be preserved intact; these were rape, assualt and battery, gambling, and liquor offenses. And the three kinds of murder, while to the courts (and defendants) quite distinct, to the historian are fairly minor variations on a specific kind of interpersonal violence. The theft category deviates in one case, that of robbery, from the view of theft in nineteenth century Ohio, for the Secretary of State considered robbery to be a crime against the person, rather than a crime against property.

Theft by trick is a distinction which I created on the basis of the historical development of the concept of theft. A major portion of the history of the law of theft is the expansion of the law over a period of 400 years to include the various forms of theft which did not involve the direct taking of someone else's property. As Jerome Hall has shown in his classic study, *Theft, Law, and Society*, this expansion of the law's coverage followed closely the needs of the growing and changing economy of England.[18] Therefore, I hypothesized that in the modern city, theft by trick would be committed by very different groups under different circumstances than theft which involved the direct taking of another's goods. Theft by trick includes those crimes where the offender exploits institutional arrangements designed to facilitate business and extend credit among strangers. All these crimes require sophistication and understanding of the business system, and all represent a significant threat to the smooth functioning of modern urban business.

The final grouping of crimes against statute, to preserve the nineteenth century terms, tends to read like a catalog of urban sins, which is what it was intended to catch. These crimes, reported by the Secretary of State with the liquor and gambling offenses, are all crimes without victims in the traditional sense, which often meant that their prosecution depended more on the law enforcement mechanism's aggressiveness than did other kinds of crime. We might say that all these crimes were moral offenses, the morality transgressed being that of the lawmakers.

This crime typology is important for several reasons. For the historian, it enables past criminal behavior to be efficiently handled without losing its complexity and subtlety. In this way, it allows criminal behavior to be examined as the behavior of an otherwise anonymous element of society: history from the "bottom up" can be written about one aspect of behavior. As elites may be studied through legislative behavior, so the bottom part of society may be studied through criminal behavior. Elites very seldom end up in the criminal courts: every exception creates a sensation—the Parkman murder in Boston, for instance. Although this study is a slight beginning, the classification scheme devised here allows an otherwise unmanageable mass of information to be digested without resorting to contemporary FBI categories or the nineteenth century categories of crimes against person, property, and statute.

Figure 1 shows the crime rates per 10,000 population for the whole state of Ohio in all years for which consistent data were published. A glance at these graphs indicates that most crime rates (per capita) display considerable stability between 1867 and 1891 with the exception of the statutory offenses, which declined, and rape, which increased slightly.

Although perhaps not too exciting in themselves, these findings run contrary to all published studies of nineteenth century crime, which find "serious" crime rates, with the exception of rape, decreasing and "minor" crime rates increasing.[19] In fact, one historian, Roger Lane, was led on the basis of his findings to conclude that urban/industrial growth was the cause of this decrease in major crime and increase in minor crime which he had discovered.[20] These differing findings for crime trends have three alternative explanations: either the rates found in previous studies are inaccurate; or the crime pattern in Ohio was atypical; or the situation in Ohio was not comparable to the eastern, older states for which the other rates have been established.

The third alternative, that Ohio cannot be directly compared to eastern states, even in the late nineteenth century, seems the most plausible to me. In the late nineteenth century there were two kinds of urban development: the developing industrial city, which was often in a transition from a pre-industrial era, and the mature industrial city. The social needs of these two kinds of urban area differ, and this is reflected in the differing emphasis on criminal prosecution and criminal behavior found in studies in the eastern United States and that of Ohio. Because the developing industrial city still emphasized

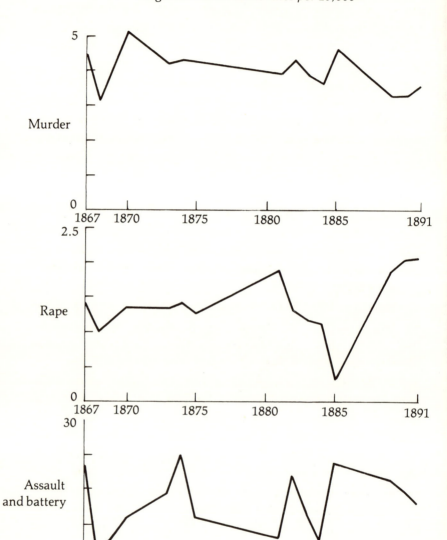

Figure 1. Ohio crime rates per 10,000[a]

Figure 1 (cont.)

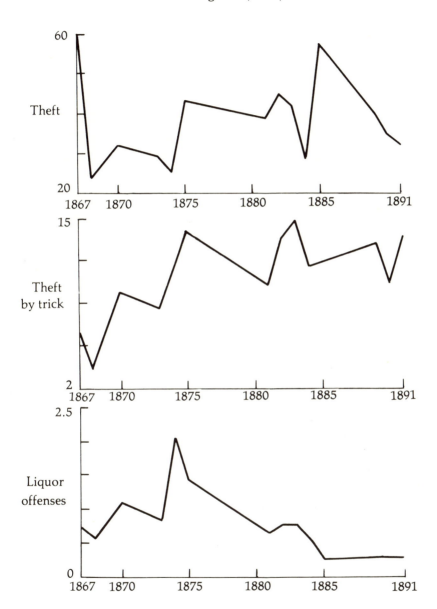

continued

Figure 1 (cont.)

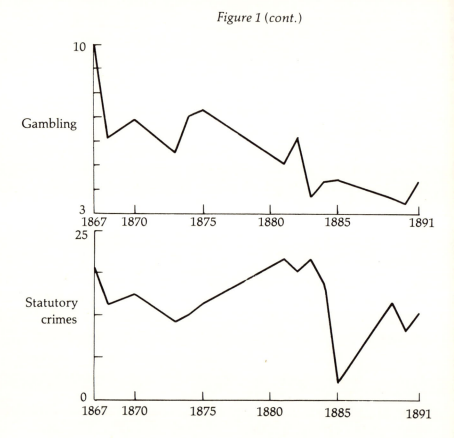

aThe data used in these graphs are from the years 1867, 1868, 1870, 1873, 1874, 1875, 1881, 1882, 1883, 1884, 1885, 1889, 1890, 1891.

face-to-face relationships, small-craft industry where the producer knew the consumer and employer-employee relationships were on a more personal level, it was characterized by the traditional crimes against property and person—theft and murder. The mature industrial city, on the other hand, with its emphasis on more secondary relationships and impersonal daily business, stressed the less direct criminal behavior such as theft by trick and offenses against public morality.

If we accept this model, then the differences between the state of Ohio and the East reflected in crime trends may be attributed to the more mature industrial development of the East. The correlations of crime rates later in this chapter also tend to support this argument about the effects of industrialization. We must therefore modify Roger Lane's interesting hypothesis that cities "civilize" their inhabitants. Instead, we must conclude that at some point in their development, cities go through changes in their crime patterns which decrease the incidence and prosecution of traditional and direct forms of criminal behavior.

As this study is concerned with poverty as well as crime, an attempt was made to develop some sort of poverty measure from the *Annual Report*. The only published measure is the number of persons in the county infirmaries (the euphemism officially given by the legislature in 1851 to what had been called poorfarms). As with the criminal data, three-year averages were established, but there were no quickly visible reasons for the fluctuations of this measure. And, as none of the analysis in this chapter found any meaningful variation in this figure, we must conclude that poorfarms provided no useful poverty measure. And probably with good reason. For the number of residents in these institutions depended on county finances, not on the number of paupers in the county. Further, their capacity at any given point of the year gives no sense of turnover—the number of persons aided yearly. And perhaps equally important, we have no statistics of outdoor relief, which probably would have been a better measure of the number of persons requiring public aid. Finally, unlike the county courts, all of which had professional clerks and an emphasis on careful record keeping, the superintendent of each infirmary was called upon to supply the state with statistics, no doubt an unwelcome and perhaps even politically dangerous chore.

The Measured Relationship of Crime to Urbanization and Industrialization

The most appropriate way to explore the relationship of crime and poverty to the various urban/industrial and agricultural/hinterland measures is through the use of correlation techniques. Regression analysis correlates one dependent variable with an independent variable, and multiple regression analysis correlates several independent variables to one dependent variable. Here, the dependent variables are the eight crime rates and the poverty rate, while the independent variables range from twelve measures used in the factor

33

analysis to the factors themselves. While simple regression analysis does give some reliable correlations, none of them is as useful or interpretable as the results given by the multiple regression analysis. (See Table 3 for an example.) Table 6 gives the results of the multiple regression. In Table 6, R represents the correlation coefficient between the crime on the left-hand side of the table and the urban and agricultural independent variates in the center of the table. The larger the value of R, the more closely correlated are the dependent and independent variables. Theft, for instance, is highly related to urbanization with $R = .44$. The BETA number in the middle column shows the relative contribution of the independent variates to the R. For example, in the poverty correlation for 1870, even though it is inverse the hinterland variate shows the most strength with a BETA of -.29 followed by the agricultural variate with a BETA of .12. Each of the

Table 6.   Multiple regression results

| | | BETA (Contribution of each variate) | | | |
| | Multiple | Urban | Hinterland | Agriculture | |
Dependent variable	R	(Variate 1)	(Variate 2)	(Variate 3)	Significance
1870					
Poverty	.32	-.04	-.29	.12	.05
Murder	.32	.32	.01	.01	.05
Assault and battery	.18	-.11	-.13	-.05	ns
Rape	.17	-.08	.07	.13	ns
Theft	.44	.31	.09	.30	.01
Trick theft	.12	.10	-.05	.02	ns
Gambling	.25	-.02	-.21	.13	ns
Liquor	.35	-.17	-.27	.14	.01
Statutory crime	.35	.14	.29	-.13	.02
1880					
Poverty	.12	-.08	.08		ns
Murder	.17	.10	-.14		ns
Assault and battery	.10	-.09	-.05		ns
Rape	.18	.15	-.08		ns
Theft	.29	.24	-.16		.03
Trick theft	.28	.26	-.09		.04
Gambling	.06	-.03	.05		ns
Liquor	.17	-.15	-.08		ns
Statutory crime	.13	.03	-.12		ns

variates was made from the factors extracted earlier in the book, and for a thorough explanation of their meaning, one should look at the second section of this chapter. The last column in Table 6 labeled Significance, shows the statistical significance of each correlation or *R*. Any significance value smaller than .05 is considered meaningful or nonaccidental.

The results are somewhat surprising. In 1870 four crimes did not relate to urbanization, while in 1880 six showed no relationship. Assault and battery, gambling and rape do not relate to urbanization for either 1870 or 1880, demonstrating the ubiquity of these three kinds of crime. Stated more precisely, the causal influence of the major factors accounted for in this book, urban/industrialism and marginal/hinterland agriculture, is not significant for three kinds of crime—assault and battery, rape, and gambling. Since these crimes do not relate to the social ecology of nineteenth century Ohio, it must be concluded that they were evenly committed and prosecuted across the state.

Another crime, theft by trick, does not correlate with high significance for 1870. This was the one crime which I had predicted to be specifically urban, for theft by trick has three necessary conditions which could best be found in urban society. These are: the need for an environment where economic transactions take place with strangers; the need for thieves who are sophisticated enough to manipulate this environment; and the threat such theft would impose on a dominant society which depends on the security of nonpersonal economic transactions. There are two alternative reasons to explain theft by trick's failure to correlate: either the above hypothesis is wrong or Ohio's urban/industrial areas had not developed to the degree required to provide the necessary conditions.

However, by 1880 the social structure had changed. And the multiple regression for theft by trick tends to confirm the second explanation—the lack of urban social development in 1870—possibly one of the more exciting insights of this analysis. For by 1880 the correlation coefficient (*R*) for theft by trick had risen to .28, significant above the .05 level, with the major explanatory contribution coming from the urban/industrial measure. This change in *R* argues for an important change in the nature of at least some Ohio cities between

1870 and 1880. Ohio's urban places were becoming more modern or mature, conforming more closely to our own perception of the social nature of the city. Theft by trick in one decade had become an urban crime.

Poverty, which correlates strongly and significantly for 1870, mainly because of its inverse relationship to hinterland counties, does not correlate significantly in 1880. As previously mentioned, the nature of the poverty measure, constructed from the number of persons in the poorhouses, may have more to do with county finances and building capacity than with the number of persons needing assistance. Because the nature of the hinterland measure has changed from a combination of poor farming areas and urban hinterlands to hinterlands alone, we must attribute the change in poverty correlation to the filtering out of those areas with the truly failing farm efforts. Only a disaggregation of the data and a more detailed analysis of the nature of marginal farming could provide the answers to this problem.

In 1880 murder is no longer an urban crime, a dramatic change from 1870 when it was clearly urban, the urban variate showing the most predictive power in the equation. Murder, it must be remembered, is the most consistently reported and prosecuted crime, making our observations of its increase or decrease the most reliable of any utilized here. The end of murder as an urban crime in this decade supports the hypothesis that as urbanization and industrialization affected more deeply the social system of Ohio, secondary relationships would increase and crimes of serious interpersonal violence would decrease. Further, this supports the contention that Ohio went through a critical decade in the 1870s, a decade of modernization. As the decrease in the urban correlate of murder occurred, the urban crime of theft by trick increased; Ohio's urban places were shedding their frontier skin for a new metropolitan shape.

That murder should decrease with urbanization in the late nineteenth century is ironic, for the social cause of its decrease is just what urban critics both then and now consider to be the worst aspect of urban life—anonymity. As the face to face relationships and close family ties of the small community disappeared, so did one of the most disapproved criminal offenses, murder. One must wonder about murder today, for if it was decreasing in the late nineteenth century city, why is it on the increase now? Does this indicate that we have adapted well to city life, that social relationships are changing back to the ways of the village and family, that in fact the modern urban/industrial society is moving more toward close social relations and away from the disintegrated city of the nineteenth century?

The four studies of eastern crime cited previously also indicated that murder was decreasing with urbanization, although only Waldo Cook's study on murders in Massachusetts for 1871-92 provided a direct measure of this. Cook showed that urban areas had proportionally less murder, while rural areas with stable or declining populations had the highest murder rates. Therefore, the decreasing association of murder and urbanization in Ohio provides confirmation of the state's changing and maturing urban culture—its urban criminals were beginning to resemble those of more urban and industrial Massachusetts.

Theft remains the most highly correlated urban crime for both periods, even though its R drops from .44 to .29. For both 1870 and 1880 the contributions of the urban and hinterland measures remain the same, the urban measure accounting for most of the variation. But the lack of a third variate in 1880 to compare to 1870 makes difficult a deeper analysis of any changes that may have occurred. We can observe that theft consistently associates with urban/industrial areas and seems relatively unaffected by the changes in the urban structure that affected several of the other crimes. This means that the changes in the social structure of the city which allow the increase of theft by trick and the decrease of murder do not greatly affect the most elemental economic crime—theft. One question this raises is whether or not these different crimes were committed by different groups; did the robber also become a forger, or did new skills in criminal trades develop to send the old thieves to the poorfarm? We cannot answer this question here, but the individuals analyzed in Chapter 4 should give us some clues.

The complex of statutory crimes was designed to be a catch-all of urban related crimes as it included almost all the traditional sins of the city. However, for both 1870 and 1880 this prediction appears to be incorrect. In 1870 the R is a strong .35, but the contribution of the urban measure is slight compared to the hinterland measure. Were the evils of cities being resisted in nearby counties? And for 1880 the variable does not even have a statistically significant R. Why was the prediction so far off? We cannot conclude that the crimes which make up this variable did not actually occur in urban places, and at this point we can only observe that these crimes were not heavily prosecuted. One wonders if these statutory crimes were overlooked by the law because their threat to society was not directly economic, because those with outraged moral sensibilities do not have the same avenging diligence as other kinds of victims, or because cities were pluralistic and tolerant.

Conclusions and Summary

No simple measure of urban/rural differences turned out to be acceptable, and to analyze such things meaningfully factor analysis and the mapping of the derived factors was necessary. For this study, then, urban did not mean the five largest cities in the state, nor did rural mean counties with large farms. Instead, as such concepts involved several measures, from the size of farms to the density of population to number of child workers, a multivariate measure of "urbanness" was created through the use of factor analysis. And this complex measurement was then compared to crime rates.

When overall crime rates were examined, no dramatic trends were encountered, a finding which is contrary to studies done on eastern states at this time. Apparently Ohio had not reached the point in urban and industrial development when it could be compared to the eastern states. For the purposes of this study, such a situation is ideal, for it confirms that the socioeconomic development of Ohio was in a transition phase to the modern urban/industrial era.

The correlation analysis shows several things about the urban structure of late nineteenth century Ohio and the relationship of this structure to crime and poverty. The most important is the finding in the crime analysis that Ohio's urban places were changing and beginning to conform to behavior patterns that we have called modern. Also important is the discovery that three crimes—assault and battery, rape, and gambling—were ubiquitous throughout the state, in agricultural as well as urban areas. And finally, we see that because urban/industrial places were modernizing, the relationship of murder, liquor prosecutions, and poverty with urban areas declined between 1870 and 1880. However, we should not conclude because of this that cities were becoming safer or more humane places to live in. Just the opposite may have been true, because the urban crimes of 1880 indicate a continuing or perhaps growing attack on property.

The substantive conclusions are only a part of this chapter, however, for it also demonstrates the possibilities inherent in published data for sophisticated research. All the data were derived from the published U.S. census or the *Annual Reports* of the Secretary of State of Ohio. The possibilities have only been touched here, and similar or better data exists for other states. The information that local governments saw fit to publish still remains a rich lode for historians. We only need to put our modern analytic tools to work.

3 • Crime in Franklin County, 1859-1885

Wherever men and women are herded together, as in the poor and squalid portions of large cities, or great numbers are employed at special work, as in our manufacturing towns, there will be found those influences which make criminals of men, and even more surely of women.

Eliza M. Mosher, M.D. (1882)

In the previous chapter I made a large, statistical, overview of the whole state, but here the focus is narrower, showing in greater detail just one county. While the previous statewide analysis emphasized statistical manipulation as the means of making sense of published data from two sources, the state and federal governments, this chapter uses the records of one criminal court from one county, records which furnish much more detail about more cases than the state summaries. This chapter should be seen as the halfway point between the macro-analysis of the previous chapter and the microanalysis of individuals in the following chapter. There are theoretical, substantive, and methodological reasons for proceeding in this fashion. Chapter 2 treated counties by comparing their degree of urbanization and amount of crime over two different time periods, covering 1867-83, but without following year by year time changes. Thus, the previous chapter corresponds to two cross-sectional slices of a large place, Ohio, while this chapter forgoes cross-sectional scale in favor of examining one county only as it urbanized over a twenty-five year period of time, Columbus growing from 38 percent of the county's population in 1860, to 49.6 percent in 1870 and to 59.5 percent in 1880. The methodological reasons parallel the theoretical: Chapter 2 used the data published by the Secretary of State of Ohio annually, data submitted to him by the county clerks of court, but this chapter moves one step closer to local conditions by using the county court records themselves, without benefit of abstraction by the clerk. And the chapter following this one moves in even closer, examining individuals who appeared in the court records.

The chapter is organized into five parts, preceeded by a discussion of the data and methodology. In the first part crime rates are discussed in a manner comparable to the crime rates in Chapter 2; the second part examines rates of specific crimes which have not been cast into typologies, for instance, resisting an officer. In the third part other aspects of criminal defendants, such as sex and plea patterns, are analyzed, and the fourth looks at the behavior of the court itself, for example, methods of punishment prescribed. The fifth summarizes the whole chapter. The reader uninterested in research problems is advised to proceed directly to the first part.

All the data relating to the first identificatation of a criminal act has been derived from one source, the Franklin County Criminal Docket. In actuality, Franklin County did not have (and does not have) a separate criminal court, but fortunately, for administrative purposes the docket recorded all criminal cases. Fortunate, because as Table 7 shows, several courts often had concurrent or contradictory jurisdiction. The county level courts had jurisdiction over all major crimes and felonies, while local courts tried misdemeanors. There are both gains and losses in analyzing only serious offenses. While we lose such crimes as drunkenness or reckless (buggy) driving, we gain in the legal selection of only more serious crimes and criminals.

Although not a perfect device for the historian, the court that tried major crimes and felonies served as a sampling agency with the virtue of consistency, and what we have lost in the cross-section of misdemeanant activity has been offset by an important degree of accuracy. The basic formats of most nineteenth century court dockets are similar to one another, although there is some variation in detail from county to county or state to state. The information includes the defendant's name, the charge, an entry date (which is usually not the day of arrest but the date the court was informed of the arrest), the date when recognizance was given (if it was), the amount of bail, the plea, the adjudication, the sentence, the name of the judge and jurors, if any, and the county's costs for the trial. In other words, the docket

Table 7. Criminal jurisdiction of Ohio courts

Year	Common Pleas Court (County)	Probate Court (County)	District Court	Circuit Court	Supreme Court
1802	All crimes except for capital offenses →				Served as annual county court, trying all capital offenses →
1851	Judges elected, no longer appointed	Overlapping jurisdiction with Common Pleas. Seems to have been for nonserious crimes; i.e., riot, petit larceny, etc.	Appellate court from Common Pleas. Same original jurisdiction as Supreme Court. Inoperative by 1865		Ceased to be county court. Became court of last resort, meeting annually →
1853	Given capital offense jurisdiction also →				
1862			→		
1883				Succeeded District Courts ↓	
1912				Became County Appeals Court	

was created not as a record of criminal behavior but as a bookkeeping account for an institution of public policy. And it is this accountant mentality of the records which benefits us, for this mentality encouraged if it did not guarantee a high degree of consistency, removing the records from the arena of courtroom battle.

The format of the docket does not come without a cost, and the cost to us is the lack of detail of the incidents. But the lack of detail does serve as a healthy reminder that we are never really studying deviant behavior so much as we are stuyding the application of criminal definitions by the dominant social groups.[1] The only reason the defendant's name is in the records at all is to preserve a list of official deviants, a kind of roll call of what Harold Garfinkel calls "degradation ceremonies."[2] Other than being a list of officially labeled criminals, the dockets are mere bookkeeping devices for the state: lest we begin to think fear of the individual criminal was a dominant theme in the Franklin County Courts, the dockets quickly show in their format that crime very much is determined by the effort and money the dominant society is willing to put forth. The more money and the more effort, the more crime; when examining official records, we should think of them as a list of crimes purchased by society. From the point of view of the courts and the society they represent, a list of jury names and court costs is more important than such information as the defendant's age, residence, or other socially defining characteristics.

Before we begin to look at the data in the criminal dockets, we should establish clearly what the dockets represent. They do not represent a mirror of criminal activity or even of court activity, but the result of a complex system of interactions, only a few of which we can measure and analyze. The main interest in this book is the behavior of those persons who became defined, even if momentarily, by the dominant society as criminals, and the court record is the indicator of this two-sided interaction. This chapter is not especially concerned with innocence or guilt, nor is much of this book, because the question of innocence or guilt in itself is not closely related to criminal behavior.

Guilt or innocence is more an aspect of the operation of the court system as, for instance, are court costs. Instead, my assumption is that the entry of an individual's name in the criminal docket stigmatizes that person as a probable criminal—a criminal who may be innocent or guilty, but still a criminal. From what we know about the operations of the criminal courts in present times, this is not an absurd definition, but closely conforms to practice. My assumption is that, in general, for a person's name to be entered on the criminal docket, the person was by that action socially defined as a potential member of the criminal class. As this book is concerned with the criminal class, its behavior, and its characteristics, this mark alone should be enough definition; if an analysis of adjudications proves otherwise, they can be read as a refinement of the definition of the criminal class, but until such a situation becomes apparent, we will continue to assume that the mere fact of entry in the criminal record is a sign of membership. And more to the point, for the purposes of the analysis of crime rates, not individuals, this argument is not especially worrisome, for it is safe to assume that though a specific individual may not have been guilty, the offense was still committed by someone.

For this study, I coded all crimes entered in the criminal dockets of Franklin County, from the beginning of the dockets in June 1859 up through October 1885. As the ultimate object of interest is the criminal defendant more than the court or the incidence of crime, an entry was made for each defendant, rather than for each criminal offense. Because there were about 500 crimes which were committed by more than one person, one might see the total number of crimes as being exaggerated. For example, if ten persons were arrested for playing baseball on Sunday, I entered the offense ten times, rather than once.[3] Argument over which is more "real" is, I feel, pointless; as our concern is with the "dangerous class" and their place in society, individual offenders provided the basic data.

Roughly 180 cases per year were coded for this study, a total of 4,514 in all. These include 139 criminal offenses, ranging from "swearing obscenely" to murder. Some problems arose in moving from the state level analysis to the county level because of the classification structure used in the *Annual Reports* which provided the basic data source for Chapter 2—a structure which must be retained here for the sake of comparability between the whole state of Ohio and Franklin county. The difficulties involved in compromising between too much specificity and complete comparability with the state *Reports* have forced me to analyze the crime rates from two points of view—in the first part, with complete comparability to the state rates in Chapter 2, and in the second part, from a point of view specific only to Franklin county with some of the more detailed categories retained. Inevitably, some of the more curious and amusing crimes were unusable for analytic purposes, mainly because they were unique—for instance, "stoning the house of one John McCann."

It is important to get some sense of the relationship between Franklin County crime as it appeared in the official state statistics and as it appeared in the pages of the criminal docket. This helps give a feel for the county and provides a critique of the *Annual Report's* reliability. Figure 2 contains a set of six graphs, one for each crime category with two lines, one representing the crime rates published in the *Annual Report*, the other the crime rates found in the dockets. To achieve comparability, the official state-reported rates were lagged by one year. One breathes a sigh of relief to discover that, in general, the rates tend to parallel one another—a finding that gives more reliability to the analysis of crime over the whole state in the preceding chapter.

Figure 2. Crime rates: Franklin County as reported by the state and as found in the dockets, 1866-69, 1880-84

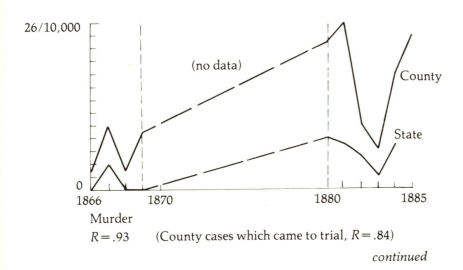

26/10,000

(no data)

County

State

0

1866　1870　1880　1885

Murder

R = .93 　(County cases which came to trial, R = .84)

continued

Figure 2 (cont.)

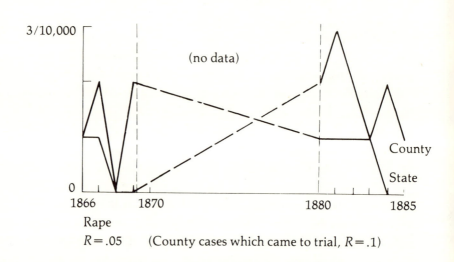

Rape

$R = .05$ (County cases which came to trial, $R = .1$)

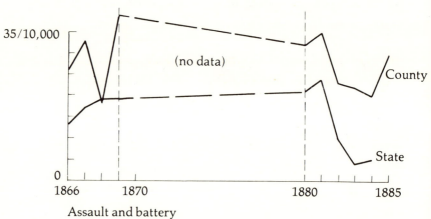

Assault and battery

$R = .66$ (County cases which came to trial, $R = .70$)

Figure 2 (cont.)

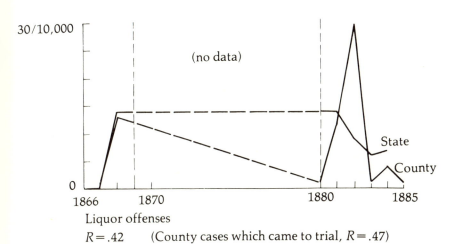

Liquor offenses
$R = .42$ (County cases which came to trial, $R = .47$)

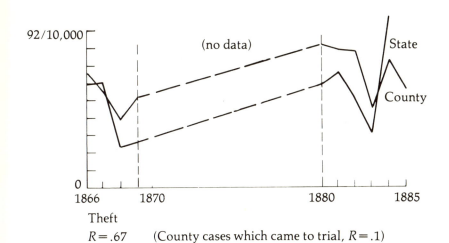

Theft
$R = .67$ (County cases which came to trial, $R = .1$)

continued

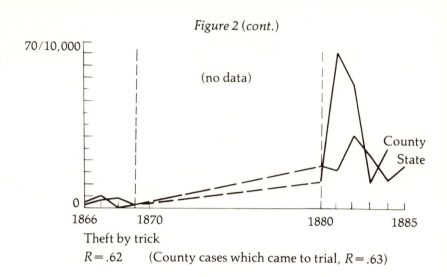

Figure 2 (cont.)

Theft by trick

$R = .62$ (County cases which came to trial, $R = .63$)

To provide a statistical confirmation of the visual impression given by the graphs for the two versions of the crime rates, the correlation coefficient (Pearson's R) was calculated for years with comparable data. The correlation coefficient was also calculated for country rates of only those crimes coming to trial—an attempt to reproduce the Secretary of State's data. These statistics are included with each graph. In general, either method of looking at the county data gave similar results, with the prominent exception of theft, which correlates dramatically better using the raw county data. Of course, these figures should all correlate perfectly, but the fact that there are so many high correlations is moderately reassuring. While not without error, the Secretary of State was close to accuracy. Nor is the lack of correlation for rape rates discouraging, for the total number of cases is so small that the delay of a trial for more than one year would throw off any statistic.

There are other obvious discrepancies to be observed between the two data sources. First, the official, published crime rate is much lower than that found in the county dockets, a problem for which there is an easy explanation. The Secretary of State was only interested in those crimes which came to trial, about 30 percent of all criminal cases in Franklin County. This accounts for the differences in magnitude between the two sets of rates, but has more serious consequences for comparing the rates—when over two thirds of the offenses are eliminated, often categories cannot be analyzed because so few cases were reported. This meant that while such categories as "malicious destruction of property" had to be dropped from the analysis of the state data, they can be retained for the study of Franklin County.

The second obvious discrepancy occurs in all the graphs but the one for murder—a crime, we must remember, which tends to be consistently discovered and prosecuted. How can we account for the state version of rapes, which shows an increase from 1869 to 1881, and then a sharp drop in 1884? Or the sharp increase of theft by trick which the state showed between 1880 and 1883? There are two reasons for these divergences. First, the time it took for some cases to come to trial was surprisingly long—42 percent of all crimes were not disposed of until after a year, and one fourth took two or more years after the recording of the offenses. This means that the apparent rape spree of the early eighties merely represents a spree on the part of the court, catching up with the defendants and old business. And if the lag between criminal offense and trial does not account for these apparent inconsistencies, then clerical errors and printing errors probably account for the rest.

These problems make it clear that the use of three-year averages in the previous chapter helped to eliminate wild fluctuations due to trial bunching. But, it is also clear that the published data simply are not the most sensitive indicator of crime trends and that the only close analysis of crime must be conducted from the lowest level possible: here, the court records. As the eminent criminologist, Thorsten Sellin, has said: "The value of criminal statistics as a basis for the measurement of criminality in geographic areas decreases as the procedure takes us farther away from the offence itself."[4] This serves to remind us that we never, even in the twentieth century, can measure actual criminal behavior, but only various indicators of it.[5]

Crime Rates

Considered in gross terms, the urban and industrial growth of Columbus resulted in the opposite of the predicted increase in crime. Through the period studied the overall rate of crime in Franklin County tended to decrease or stay level. As the first graph in Figure 3 shows, the peak in crime occurred in 1865—353 arrests for felonies per

Figure 3. Franklin County crime rates per 10,000 population

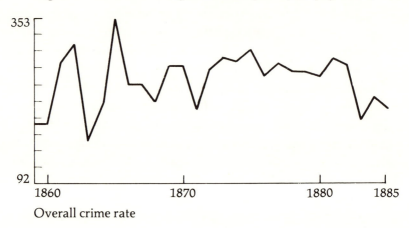

Overall crime rate

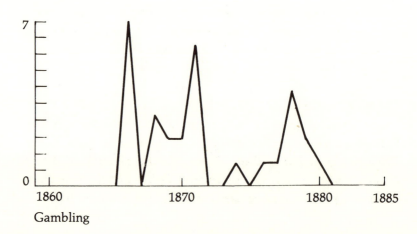

Liquor offenses

Gambling

Figure 3 (cont.)

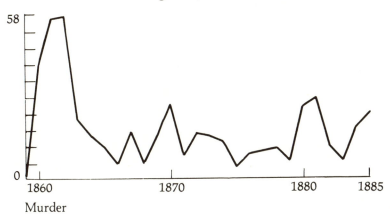

Murder

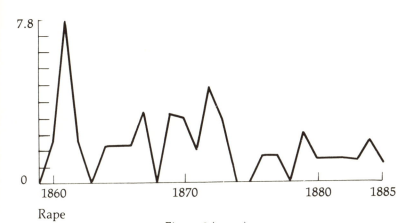

Rape

Figure 3 (cont.)
Franklin County crime rates per 10,000

Theft

continued

Figure 3 (cont.)

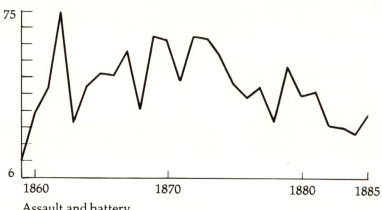

Assault and battery

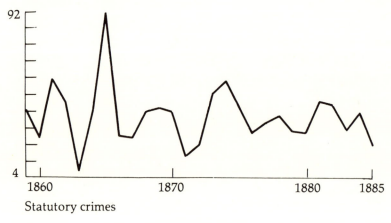

Statutory crimes

Theft by trick

10,000 persons. After this peak, there was a sharp decline in criminal activity, followed by a very slight rising trend through the early 1870s and then a decline through 1885. It is not until the overall crime pattern is broken down by kinds of crime that the effects of urbanization become apparent.

When the rates for the eight major types of crime are graphed for the period 1860-85, four distinct pattern groups emerge. (See Chapter 2 for a discussion of how these types were arrived at.)[6] Liquor and gambling offenses each stand alone, incomparable to the other crimes, and apparently fluctuating in response to unknown pressures. In the second group, murder and rape show the same basic trends—a high period in the Civil War years, followed by a drop to a stable rate through 1885. In the third group—composed of the overall crime rate, assault and battery, and theft—there is a curve peaking through the 1870s with a downward turn in the late seventies and early eighties. And in the fourth group—theft by trick and the statutory crimes—there is a general increase throughout the period, thus making this the only set of truly rising rates.

Only a quick glance at the line graphs for liquor and gambling violations is necessary to establish the obvious—there are no trends in these crime rates. Mainly this is a result of the low total number of prosecutions combined with the apparently specific causes for any set of offenses. These rates will respond only to an analysis through the newspapers and even then will not tell us about the aggregate behavior of the criminal class of Franklin County. As it stands, we must simply conclude that the not very serious offenses of liquor and gambling violations were sporadically prosecuted, probably from the influence of local pressure groups such as the temperance movement or local religious leaders like Washington Gladden.

The other crime trends are not so glibly dismissed. Each group has patterns and causes which are worth speculating upon. Murder and rape follow the most predictable pattern of these four groups, a pattern which has been commented upon by other historians.[7] This pattern is characterized by a sharp increase in interpersonal violence during and after the Civil War, similar to the alleged increase in violence after the Revolutionary War. After the period of the war-engendered violence, the two crime rates stay steady through the eighties. This pattern represents the interplay of two separate causes. The stable period after the war outburst represents "normality," for our previous analysis showed that neither murder nor rape were especially sensitive to social conditions, while the violence during the war represented the conflict between the values of war itself and the values of the society that engages in war. Both those who had fought or were fighting in the war as well as those who took advantage of the looser social control during the war ended up being arrested for assault and battery more often than in nonwar times. Thus the Civil War meant violence even outside of battle.

Certainly this war-engendered "crime wave" needs more examination than I can provide here. But let us imagine the situation in Columbus and the surrounding hinterland: the whole of the county had about 53,000 people, and the city of Columbus had about 30,000. The Civil War had been going on for almost three years; first volunteers were returning and the draft had begun. Women's groups were making bandages and lint to send to the military. The town was filled with patriotic fervor, perhaps waning a bit, and the Ohio State Penitentiary, just outside the city limits, held Confederate prisoners of war. At least, this is how the local histories picture the scene. But, perhaps for the people who composed the dangerous class things were not seen in quite the same way. For them the war meant economic hardship, loss of young men, either permanently or temporarily, and an increase in the demand for the services they provided to the city—prostitution, illegal liquor, gambling. For the dominant society, the perceived chaos of war altered their relationship with the dangerous class; what might be peccadillos in low stress times suddenly loomed as threats to the social order in wartime. Thus for both the law breakers and the law enforcers, the Civil War created a social situation conducive to a crime wave.[8]

As the basis for the crime wave was not enduring, that is, it depended on continuing inability to adjust to the demands of war by the dangerous class, it came to a rather quick ending. In fact, in a society working to make war, prosecuting criminals is an extra burden, requiring tax money and personnel. The average court costs were $21.50 per case in 1859, but had climbed to $37.10 in 1863. This high rate clearly was intolerable, for costs had fallen to $17.70 per case in 1865.[9]

Crime did not pay as far as the court was concerned: it incurred high costs, and the society could not afford to continue with a crime wave.

Unlike murder and rape, theft and assault and battery did not stay steady after the war. Instead both rates curve from a low point following the war to a peak in the seventies and a new low by the mid-eighties. These rates follow a twenty-year swing, the peak of which coincides with the depression of 1873-74. Clearly the peak years are attributable to the depression, but the twenty-year swing is another question.

Although it is not testable, my hypothesis is that this swing represents the convergence of two things—first, the economic pressures of the depression, and second, the more basic effects of the industrialization and urbanization of the county, the increased social and economic pressures necessitating a process of social adjustment on the part of the marginal workers. The effects of the depression can never be examined closely with the available data, for correlation can never be proved to show causation. On the other hand, when the criminals themselves are examined in the next chapter, it may be that their occupational and social status will demonstrate whether or not marginal workers were in fact responsible for the increase in theft and assault and battery.

Thefts which depended on trick and deception, crimes which the previous chapter has shown to be highly correlated with urban and industrial areas in the state, show a pattern dramatically different from all other crimes. The rate for this group of crimes, which includes embezzlement, forgery, frauds, and obtaining money or goods under false pretences, is steady and quite low until about 1870, when it suddenly zooms. This rise clearly demonstrates the urban nature of thefts by deception and functions as an indicator of the change and urbanization occurring in Columbus. As one might predict, the thefts by trick continued to soar, past the period selected for this study, on into the decade of the nineties. Not until the late nineties did this crime group stabilize, and when it did so, the rate was considerably higher than the pre-1870 era.[10] Indeed, by 1885 Columbus was experiencing a veritable crime wave of frauds, embezzlements, forgeries, and thefts by false pretences. No doubt, as Columbus entered the age of massive urbanization, the city needed and used this crime wave as a method of redefining the boundaries of acceptable behavior. Crime waves, as Kai Erickson has suggested for colonial Americans, served a society undergoing changes for which it had not been prepared, and only through the burst of criminal prosecutions for theft which depended on the victim mistakenly trusting the offender could the city rationalize and control its new size and changed basis of social interactions.[11] More direct crimes, which required little skill or training, did not fit into the increasingly complex urban culture as well as before. And this raises a question which cannot be answered until the next chapter—were the same kinds of people arrested for these very different kinds of crimes, or did they originate from different sources? Although the answers provided in this study will be too narrow and case specific, the question has important implications for the study of social change and its effect on individuals: that is, are new forms of social behavior enacted by persons who have changed their roles to fit the needs of a changing society, or do the new forms recruit people from totally unrelated segments of society? Are yesterday's horse thieves today's car thieves?

Unreduced Crime Rates

We can get closer to the particulars of criminal behavior than the eight types of crime discussed above. There were 139 different charges found in the 25 years surveyed, but because many involved only a few cases, there is little sense in trying to find their change in incidence over time. The others are of interest, either because they are unique or because they allow us an insight which grosser classifications obscure. I will look at twenty of these crimes here, the first two with the purpose of checking the validity of the previous eight-fold crime typology and the others for their own merits.

Assault with Intent to Kill and Assault with Intent to Rape. Both of these crime categories involve intent, a fact which makes them both conceptually difficult to handle: are they attempted murder or just assault, rape, or just lascivious assault? More confusing, does the addition of intent to the criminal definition indicate court behavior or criminal behavior; does it indicate plea bargaining of a more serious charge or the court's upping of a lesser charge to ensure conviction? Often these questions are unanswerable with our present data, which leads to conceptual difficulties.

One way of understanding this problem is by simply comparing the rates over time to answer the simple question: do they approximate or highly correlate with one another? Assault and battery does not correlate significantly with assault with intent to kill ($R = -.10$). While, on the other hand, assault with intent to kill does correlate highly with murder, either indicating that the intent was real ($R = .97$) or that the two forms of violence were in response to similar social conditions. Assault with intent to rape, on the other hand, does not correlate quite as highly with rape ($R = .44$), but this is very probably the result of the low number of cases. The significance of these relationships, then, is in the differentiation between the forms of personal violence, murder versus assault and battery, indicating that to lump them together as "crimes against the person," as so often happened in nineteenth century criminal statistics, is misleading and obscures trends.

Prepolitical Crimes of Rebellion. Seven different crime categories seem to me to have related meaning—all constitute aspects of the kinds of crimes which the English historian E. J. Hobsbawm has often discussed; all are a form of prepolitical violence. Such crimes involve the attempts of people without access to the power structure to affect and control various aspects of their social or economic life. Although there are not any offenses which specifically have such content in the dockets, there are several which were at least possibly prepolitical protest. These are: resisting an officer, riot, destroying property, destroying a building, house stoning (literally, "stoning the house of one John McCann"), maliciously throwing down a fence, peace warrants (not really a crime), and disturbing a religious meeting. These offences are shown in Tables 8, 9, and 10.

Urban rebelliousness, however slight, did not display any clear or dramatic trends through the whole period under study. Within the twenty-five year period, there were some interesting swings. For both riot and resisting an officer, the Civil War period had a predictable excess, followed in the early seventies by a splurge of rioting charges and in the late seventies by a slighter peak in resisting charges. The depression of 1873 and 1874 immediately comes to mind in conjunction with the riot charges, but further research into qualitative sources is needed to confirm this. Rather than display the long-term effects of industrial growth, these crimes seem to have been more in response to local and specific situations.

Table 8. *Crimes of rebelliousness by five year periods* (N = 101)

Charge	1861-65	1866-70	1871-75	1876-80	1881-85
Resisting an officer	6	0	4	8	5
Riot	17	7	33	7	14

Table 9. *Crimes against property by five year periods* (N = 72)

Charge	1861-65	1866-70	1871-75	1876-80	1881-85
Destroying property	15	9	8	14	13
Destroying a building	4	0	6	0	0
Stoning a house	3	0	0	0	0

Table 10. *Fence breaking and peace warrants by five year periods* (N = 247)

Charge	1861-65	1866-70	1871-75	1876-80	1881-85
Destroying a fence	0	0	0	0	6
Peace warrants	62	36	49	38	56

On the other hand, destroying property, buildings, and house stoning do not show clear peaks but a somewhat steady incidence. This is of importance for these attacks on property often represented a second phase of prepolitical rebellion. Hobsbawm, in *Captain Swing*, shows how in 1830 the rebellious farm laborers in England first engaged in public acts of rebelliousness before they began smashing machines, the attack on property being an escalation and more directed form of violence.[12] Thus, at least in our period, we can conclude that forms of lower class rebelliousness did not change or become more advanced—a weak but persistent state of surliness existed.

The crime of fence destroying, clearly a directed and symbolic act of anger, has only 6 arrests in all, occurring after 1880. Probably related to some local incident, we can see in this example that if the second level of prepolitical violence did exist in Franklin County, it was only to a very slight degree.

Peace warrants, very often sworn out against a troublesome spouse, represent a different kind of social disorder. Rather than being directed against a group or class, they are a function of tension within a group. Unfortunately, this "crime" cannot be used as an index of such tension, because in the court records it represents two very different forces—social tension within close groups of people and the society's awareness and trust of the court system in prosecuting these tensions. Analytically, differences like these mean that even if a clear trend were visible, we could not interpret it unambiguously. That is, two totally different causes would have the same results.

Urban and Social Control Crimes. Some urban crimes arise from the tensions and opportunities of urban life, while others represent an effort on the part of the dominant social groups to control or change certain elements of developing urban industrial life. In Tables 11, 12, and 13, the dramatic raw incidences of a selected group of these crimes are displayed.

Receiving stolen goods is probably the only crime that has always been associated with urbanization. Functioning as a middleman between producer (thief) and consumer (buyer), the receiver of stolen goods has been historically hard to find, hard to arrest, and hard to charge. Jerome Hall's legal study of theft has shown how the receiving of stolen goods did not become a felony until the early nineteenth century and how legally difficult obtaining a conviction was, mainly because testimony was required of a confessed criminal offender.[13] With this in mind, it is instructive to look at Table 11 where the crime is marked by a few isolated cases before 1870, while by 1873 it increased dramatically. This matches closely the rates for theft by trick, another urban crime as we have discovered, and tends to confirm the hypothesis that Columbus experienced a change to a modern city during the 1870s.

I have included the incidence of arrests for running a house of ill fame to illustrate the difficulty of interpreting what would seem to be an indicator and aspect of urbanization—prostitution. Clearly our

Table 11. *Receiving stolen goods by five year periods* (N=64)

Charge	1861-65	1866-70	1871-75	1876-80	1881-85
Receiving stolen goods	1	3	15	26	19

Table 12. *Prostitution and picking pockets by five year periods* (N=41)

Charge	1861-65	1866-70	1871-75	1876-80	1881-85
Running a house of ill-fame	6	4	5	8	1
Picking pockets	0	0	0	0	17

Table 13. *Cutting and Sunday violations by five year periods* (N=71)

Charge	1861-65	1866-70	1871-75	1876-80	1881-85
Cutting	1	1	11	9	23
Sunday violations	0	0	1	4	21

problem in measuring prostitution is fluctuating prosecution, and the best situation (for those analyzing urban change) we could hope for is one where the city rationalized and covertly accepted prostitution, using fines and arrests as a form of control and taxation. Yet we cannot tell if that was the case in Columbus, for although the crimes seem to peak in the late seventies, the number of occurrences simply are not enough to interpret reliably. Yet we know the city had "droves of prostitutes filling High Street so full at night that decent women cannot walk unattended."[14] The census enumerators in 1870 recorded 10 houses of ill fame with a total of 42 prostitutes.[15] We can only conclude that the city had not developed to the stage where the business of prostitution would be covertly rationalized through the courts.

Picking pockets is a crime of crowds, yet Columbus, as well as the surrounding villages, must have had crowds before 1883. Whether the spurt of arrests in the mid-eighties indicates a new effort on the part of the police force or whether it means that pickpockets had become residence in the area cannot be told until the analysis of individuals in the next chapter is complete.

The increased incidence of Sunday law prosecutions in 1879 apparently never satisfied the famous minister, Washington Gladden, who, in 1891, was calling on decent citizens to "agitate, agitate!" This lack of prosecutions which irritated the minister indicates that not all the better elements of the city were so socially separated from the noisy baseball players and beer drinkers that they felt it necessary to stop their sport.

As crimes, the various forms of assault with a knife, referred to simply as cutting, are of interest for several reasons. These crimes of personal violence depend on an inexpensive tool with a capital investment in between that of simple assault and assault with a firearm. Although cutting can be conceived of as a crime of people too poor to buy a gun, it is not a crime with bare hands—it is a crime in the machine age of those who work in its poorly paid jobs. And, if we look at the incidence of cutting in Table 13, we see that like the receiving of stolen goods, cutting followed the advance of industrial growth in Columbus, climbing steadily upwards from the early 70s.

Aspects of Criminal Behavior

Although the data on the criminal defendants included in the dockets is slim, we can find out four things about individuals: the defendant's sex, whether the defendant pleaded guilty or not guilty, whether the charge was brought against a single person or a group, and whether persons fined could pay. With this meager information we can make several interesting discoveries.

Sex. I hypothesize that as a traditional society changes to an urban society, the sex composition of its criminals will change. Women, as they move from home to factory, will also move into other nontraditional roles, including criminal activities. If we examine Table 14 with this in mind, we see that the data tend to support our hypothesis. Eight percent of all criminal defendants in Franklin County were women, but there are some differences in this figure when broken

Table 14. Defendant's sex by type of offense

Charge	Men	Women	Total
Murder	302 (97.4%)	8 (2.6%)	310
Rape	28 (93.3%)	2 (6.7%)	30
Assault and battery	666 (91.6%)	61 (8.4%)	727
Theft	1,471 (93.2%)	108 (6.8%)	1,579
Theft by trick	231 (90.2%)	25 (9.8%)	256
Gambling	19 (100%)	0 (0 %)	19
Liquor violation	153 (97.5%)	4 (2.5%)	157
Statutory offense	541 (86.8%)	82 (13.2%)	623
Total	3,411 (92.2%)	290 (7.8%)	3,701

down by type of crime. Women were more often charged with theft by trick than their total participation in criminal activity warranted, and theft by trick was a major emerging urban crime. Also, women participated even more highly in the statutory crimes. Of course, this group of crimes includes prostitution, but if we subtract these offenses, the ratio is still 88 percent men to 12 percent women. At the opposite end of the spectrum, we find women are underrepresented in gambling, murder, and liquor charges. Since none of these groups of crime is markedly urban in nature, the hypothesis that women will be found moving into nontraditional roles of criminal behavior tends to be supported.

Table 15 shows the sex distributions by type of crime from 1859 to 1885, omitting those crimes that involved few women. Although we cannot say that there was a trend for more women to be charged with murder, because of the spotty distribution of cases, we can say that the incidence of women being tried did increase after 1880, but we should not attempt to interpret this because the data are lacking.

With assault and battery, the situation is different. After some wild fluctuations through the Civil War, a very slight rising trend is visible, beginning slightly before 1870 and continuing through 1885. This is remarkable when we see that there is an opposite trend for a crime which is equally traditional—theft. Here, I think, we must interpret

*Table 15. Percentage of defendants who were women
by five year intervals
(N=287)*

Crime	1861-65	1866-70	1871-76	1875-80	1881-85
All crime	13	8	6	6	8
Murder	4	0	0	0	6
Rape	0	0	33[a]	0	0
Assault and battery	7	5	10	8	10
Theft	16	9	4	5	6
Theft by trick	11	8	8	8	13
Gambling	0	8	0	0	0
Liquor offenses	13	0	3	10	0
Statutory offenses	24	10	9	12	12

[a]One of three defendants

these variations with the kind of crime in mind. Assault and battery is a crime of interpersonal violence and cannot be easily classified as a "rational" crime like theft. Often this crime represents a nongoal-oriented way of discharging tension and an inability to manipulate one's environment. Perhaps that was the case here: if the rising number of women factory workers is an indication, we can say that the changing nature of the local economy was giving rise to increased expectations on the part of women. And since these expectations most often met with frustration, violence within groups represents the first and easiest mode of expressing the resulting tension.

Of the other two crimes graphed, theft by trick shows the only clear trends. Here we see a familiar pattern: wild fluctuations throughout the war period, followed by a period of stability until an increase in the eighties. Because women are overrepresented in this crime category, it is important that we remember the structure of the crime discovered in Chapter 2. There we found that theft by trick was slightly associated with urban areas in 1870 and strongly associated with them by 1880. Thus, as the crime itself became more urban, the persons who committed it changed.

This strongly supports the hypothesis that women will move into new roles as a society becomes more urban and industrial, in this case moving into a crime which is itself nontraditional.

There are other sex differences which appear in the court dockets. For instance, women tended to plead not guilty more often than men, indicating that they either exploited their role stereotypes or that they were, indeed, less often guilty than men. Although not guilty verdicts were returned in equal numbers for both, women were more likely than men to have their case dismissed with costs or discharged. For whatever reasons then, role stereotyping, actual innocence, or more courtroom ability, women tended to get off slightly better than men.

Multiple Defendants. Often more than one person was charged with a criminal offense. Of all 4,514 criminal cases between 1860 and 1885, 28 percent were in a group of more than one defendant. Average group size fluctuated between 2 and 4 persons, but the average went over 3 persons in only 4 years—1863, 1874-75, 1879, and 1884. The percentage of crimes committed by more than one person fluctuated slightly during the period under study, with a generally rising trend until the eighties, when a slight fall-off occurred. (When this is broken down by type of crime, no startlingly different patterns emerge.) At best, we can only observe that there was a slight increase through the seventies, but without further evidence, we cannot analyze the causes or meaning of this.

Court Behavior

Although the focus of this study is on individuals and their behavior, certain aspects of the court's behavior as an institution remain of importance. Court behavior refers to the court's methods of handling criminal cases, especially those methods which are not really a result of an individual defendant's behavior. Even though the court's behavior does not explain any of the major problems or questions we are examining here, it should not be neglected, principally because our whole vision of criminal activity in Columbus is through the lens of the court records.

The dockets give several items of information for each case, depending on how far it was prosecuted, which make the record of the court's activity. There was very little formal giving of bail, but many defendants were given recognizance for a refundable fee, which functioned something like bail. The amount of this fee was recorded in the dockets, as was the court cost for each case. Also recorded was the sentencing of those defendants who were found guilty; this information included both the amount of fines, the length of the sentence, and the place of incarceration—varying from the dungeon to the penitentiary.

Court costs per case for jurors, transcripts, sheriff's fees, and so on varied from a low of $1 to a high of $1,589. Most cases were relatively inexpensive, but there were still almost 200 cases which cost over $100 to prosecute. Not too surprisingly, the cases with high costs tended to have more expensive bail, a heavier percentage of sentencing to the penitentiary, and longer sentences. Of the 39 cases costing over $200, only 3 were not found guilty.[16] Either the court only invested heavily in those cases which it was sure the state would win, or to be cynical, the court was biased toward finding guilt in expensive trials. Statistics were on the side of defendants who put up as little fight as possible, and those defendants who were able to have prolonged court battle entered a win-lose situation with the odds heavily against them.

Court costs were also oddly distributed for those cases involving women, for whom expenses never went over $200.[17] Furthermore, women were overrepresented in those cases which cost less than $10. One might expect some bias in these figures because of the different types of crime women were involved in, but when crime type is accounted for, the disproportion remains. Women apparently were prosecuted less vigorously and were unwilling or unable to carry on long court battles.

In the twenty-five years of criminal dockets which I examined, the courts employed 7 different kinds of sentence for the 1,128 cases which were adjudicated as guilty. These types of punishment included the state penitentiary, fines, the county jail, the dungeon, the reform school or industrial school, and two cases of hangings. Table 16 shows the distribution of these types of punishment by five-year intervals from 1860 to 1885. As expected of a court which tried felonies, one

Table 16. *Type of punishment by five year intervals* (N=1,113)

Punishment	1861-65	1866-70	1871-75	1876-80	1881-85
Penitentiary	35	81	111	169	168
Jail	2	27	68	106	30
Fine	19	41	66	48	34
Dungeon	19	31	16	0	19
Reform school	0	3	7	4	6
Industrial school	0	0	0	1	0
Hanging	0	0	1	0	1

half of the guilty defendants were sentenced to prison. Only two persons were sentenced to be hanged, and this out of 16 first-degree and 20 second-degree murder cases. But probably most surprising for such recent times is the court's fairly heavy usage of the dungeon as a means of punishment, often with only bread and water as sustenance. Almost 9 percent or 97 defendants were incarcerated in the dungeon during this twenty-five year period.

The court's usage of different kinds of punishment varied in response to several kinds of pressure, only a few of which can be accounted for. If the sentence types are treated as a crude continuum, from the penitentiary to the dungeon, the mean score for each year can be calculated with one representing the penitentiary and the higher numbers the less serious forms of punishment. These scores may then be charted as in Figure 4 to show the relative degree of severity of punishment used by the court over the years. There is an overall trend toward more serious punishment throughout the period, with three peaks in 1863, 1869, and 1873-74. The 1863 peak is part of the Civil War crime wave which we have observed before, while the 1873-74 peak is probably the court's reaction to the mid-seventies swing upward in most crime rates. This, of course, coincides with the depression and with the most sudden increase in Columbus's rate of industrialization. Thus these two peaks are not surprising in view of the other crime data, but what is unexpected is the overall trend toward more serious punishment throughout the period—a phenom-

Figure 4. Average sentence severity, all crimes

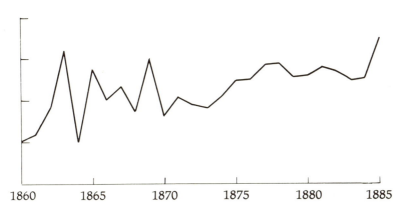

| 1860 | 1865 | 1870 | 1875 | 1880 | 1885 |

enon which does not conform to the general crime trends in the county.[18]

A disaggregation of the data complicates the matter. We see that the peak of penitentiary sentences in 1863 is partly due to the small number of convictions, while the apparent 1873-74 peak may be more the results of fines and jailings than of sentences to the penitentiary. Further, the 1874-80 period emerges as a time of heavy jailings with 1877-78 seeing heavy penitentiary sentences also. By the early eighties jailings have dropped and penitentiary sentences seem to have started a long upward climb, confirming the general trend shown in Figure 4. The court's usage of the dungeon is inconsistent with the other trends, marked by complete disuse between 1875 and 1881.

With the exception of the dungeon, these trends should be interpreted as a three stage sequence in the court's attempts to control crime. This sequence of escalating efforts began in 1870 with fines, turned by the mid-seventies to jailings and finally in the eighties began a heavy application of penitentiary sentences.

Why this apparent effort at stiffer penalties for criminal offenses? We know serious crime was holding steady through the period, and the crimes that were increasing were not perceived by the court as especially serious. Perhaps the best explanation with the available data is in court costs. As Figure 5 indicates, the decade of the seventies saw a new high plateau of criminal court costs—a plateau that did not show any signs of a dramatic decrease. Thus, even though crime rates

Figure 5. Court costs, yearly average

were not rising, the institutional pressure of costs had risen, suggesting this pressure resulted in the court's meting out of increasingly severe punishments.

Although the defendant's plea and the court's adjudication are not very interesting in themselves, they can provide some exciting insights into both the defendant's and the court's perceptions. For the purpose of this part of the analysis, we must beg the question of actual guilt, assuming all defendants for each crime type had equal chances of innocence or guilt. What this assumption means in percentage terms is difficult to express. If guilty pleas are used, then 17 percent of all criminal defendants were guilty; on the other hand, if guilty verdicts are added to the indicator, 29 percent were guilty.

The ratio of guilty pleas to guilty judgments varies widely from charge to charge. When the crimes are arranged in the form of ascending percentages of defendants pleading guilty and compared with the percentage of guilty verdicts, we would predict a parallel relationship, if our assumption that all defendants in each crime category are equally guilty is correct. But, there is a dramatic inverse relationship, with a negative correlation coefficient of $R = -.72$. Rather than abandon our assumption, we should interpret this as a measure of the defendant's and court's differing perception of the seriousness of various crimes. In other words, let us maintain our assumption that all defendants were equally guilty, but because some crimes were perceived as more serious than others, they will be pleaded or found guilty in differing degrees.

If this was so, then the pleas and verdicts represent a "seriousness" scale, with pleas reflecting the defendant's perceptions and verdicts reflecting the court's perceptions. That is, the defendants pleaded innocent to crimes they felt were serious, while the court found guilty the crimes it felt were serious. Both court and defendants agreed that rape was the most serious crime, liquor offenses and gambling the least serious. But in between these two extremes are some interesting differences. Defendants seemed to have felt that murder was more serious than theft, while the court took the opposing viewpoint. The defendants also felt that the statutory crimes were more serious than theft, while the court placed these crimes below liquor offenses in seriousness. The final perceptual difference between the two is in the relationship of theft by trick to assault and battery, the defendants seeing theft by trick as more serious, while the court interpreted it as comparable to assault and battery.

We should interpret these differences as a reflection of the attitudes of two groups, the criminals and the court, toward their society. For both the defendants and the court, rape was very serious, liquor and gambling not very serious. The different attitudes toward the two forms of interpersonal violence, murder and assault and battery, represent two views on the use of fighting as a means to resolve problems. But fighting was not allowed by the defendants to confuse the seriousness of murder, therefore the criminals saw murder as being more serious than the court did, and fighting as less serious. For the court, theft was the most serious offense next to rape, reflecting the values of the elite of an economically growing area. On the other hand, the court placed assault and battery directly below murder and even with theft by trick in seriousness. Considering the economic threat posed by theft by trick, it is strange that the court was not more severe in dealing with it; perhaps the court felt that there were not enough cases to be worried about.

If we look more carefully at the rates of pleas by offense and year, we find that the court's attitude toward theft by trick went through a dramatic change in the early seventies, with the percentage found guilty and the percentage pleading not guilty shooting upwards during the last part of this period.[19] Thus the aggregate figure has hidden a change in perceptions, a change that shows the court's and offenders' growing perceptions of the danger in the threat to society of theft by trick.

Summary

Several substantive findings of this chapter deserve to be reiterated here. First, it was discovered that overall crime rates for Franklin County stayed fairly stable throughout the period under study—with the exception of a Civil War peak and a moderate drop in the eighties. This finding conforms more with the results of studies of crime in the eastern part of the country and tends to contradict the statewide trends of the period. When the overall rate is disaggregated, some interesting trends become apparent. Assault and battery had a peak in the early seventies, followed by a peak in theft in the late seventies, which in turn was followed by a continued increase in theft by trick, which did not peak until the early 1890s. This sequence, I infer, reflects the growth and change in the urban sophistication and complexity of Columbus—theft by trick representing the truly urban criminal offense.

Further, it was found that the category of crimes that can be characterized as prepolitical forms of protest and violence showed a definite increase throughout the period, even though the total number of cases remained relatively small. Also, crimes which are specifically and traditionally urban, like receiving stolen goods or prostitution, were on the increase, especially after 1870. And the effect of the growth of the city on crime was clearly apparent in the number of women defendants—their number increasing, especially in the urban category of theft by trick. On the other hand, the entrance of women into the role of criminal was not met with severity by the court, which tended to spend less money on their trials and to find them guilty less often than men.

And finally, it was discovered that the court itself was going through some behavioral changes during this period. The average court costs per case climbed slowly, and as they did, the court became increasingly severe in its usage of punishment. The dungeon, for instance, was abandoned for almost ten years, then reintroduced in the eighties. That the court seemed more responsive to pressures other than those of a criminal nature becomes understandable when the perceptual differences between court and defendant are observed. For the court tended to see economic crimes as more threatening than did the defendants themselves, who saw crimes against persons as more serious.

Although the original hypothesis that crime would increase as Columbus grew and urbanized is not confirmed, the change of complex patterns of criminal behavior definitely showed the effects of urbanization. Subtlety and complexity, not massive upheaval, characterized the social changes fostered by urban and industrial growth.

4 • Criminals

As the population of the State increases the number of those belonging to the *crime class*, in the nature of things, also increases, and apparently in an enlarged ratio.

For an army to go to battle with every dozen soldiers under a separate and independent commander, would at once be branded as infinite folly; and yet this is substantially our existing method of fighting the *great army of criminals*, and it ought to be corrected.

Ohio Board of State Charities (1884)

It is one thing to study crime and another to study criminals. For to be concerned with the first means one focuses on the aggregate of criminal behavior, conceptually, at least, treating it as a separate entity. The previous two chapters dealt with crime from such a perspective. To study the individual offenders, rather than just their behavior, shifts the perspective dramatically. To look at offenders means that we utilize criminal behavior as a means of identification—behavior is not considered in itself but as it is tied to the individual actor. And by our assumptions, this means that the actor is the mediating agency between the larger social system that produces the criminal behavior and the behavior itself. As the criminal behavior analyzed in the two previous chapters was used as a window on the social structure of an urbanizing and industrializing area, we may, by looking at the actors, refine our "window" on society.

Almost all nineteenth century studies of crime were concerned with finding its causes in the individual criminals: criminals, it was thought, behaved abnormally, therefore there must be something abnormal about them. This attitude saw its extreme application in the works of Robert L. Dugdale, whose classic study, *The Jukes: A Study in Crime, Pauperism, Disease, and Heredity*, was published in 1877. Yet even while claiming that genetics accounted for deviant behavior,

Dugdale thought that manipulation of the social environment could change criminals.[1] The less hard-line thinkers like Ely Van De Warker tended to be even fuzzier in their analyses, claiming on the one hand that "The propensity to crime is a fixed element in human nature" but on the other that crime is an "outgrowth from the conditions of society."[2] This kind of vague thinking allowed writers to at one time find cities as the cause of crime and at another to blame drink or genetics.

Our purpose in looking at individual criminals is somewhat different, for our ultimate interest is to gain a deeper understanding of the structure of society. Here, we learn about the larger society by studying an inarticulate group of people whose defining characteristic, for us at least, is the behavior that got them into criminal court. And by learning about them we gain insights into an aspect of the nineteenth century social system which is otherwise closed to us.

This chapter is divided into three interrelated and often overlapping parts. The first part considers all criminals, trying to understand their characteristics as a group and as subgroups. The second part looks at criminals on the basis of rural and urban places of residence, while the final part examines the problem of recidivism.

Nineteenth century observers often lumped criminals together with poor people into what Charles Loring Brace called the "dangerous classes." These people, "the product of accident, ignorance, and vice," formed "great masses of destitute, miserable, and criminal persons" who, though "hidden beneath the surface" of society were ready for revolutionary outbreak at any moment.[3] Reformers had special motivations to bring the "dangerous classes" back into the mainstream of society, for the very social structure was threatened by their presence.

Those reformers and observers could not conceive that the criminal class might be an integral part of their society—a dark underside with interests conflicting with those of the dominant society. Thus, explanations of criminality were developed to help the dominant society rationalize and explain the existence of the criminals. Social theory had to put the blame on the criminals, for to do otherwise would have been to blame society.

Because of the social threat it posed, a threat akin to an enemy army if we listen to the Ohio Board of Charities, the "criminal class" did not go unexamined.[4] Early in the century statistical studies began to appear; however, these studies were flawed in two ways. First, they invariably dealt only with convicted criminals in jails and prisons, the assumption being only "real" criminals were in prison—the adjudicated guilty were the truly guilty. They were also flawed in the questions they asked, for when the study went beyond nativity or literacy it went to measures not comparable with the noncriminal society, asking such questions as "do parents drink?" or "influence of bad associates," or the like. Although such studies seem of little use to us, they were distinguished by the attention they paid to individual careers, viewing the individual's life as a series of events and decisions.

Unfortunately, we do not have access to individual life stories, only to selected events in the lives of many individuals. For criminal offenders, this event is their appearance in court. Data to discuss the process of "becoming deviant," as the criminologist David Matza calls it, will probably never be available on a wide scale for the nineteenth century. On the whole this is just as well, for it forces us to examine criminals as a part of a social system, to examine only those aspects of their lives which can be compared to the total population. And the information on individuals is available in amazingly unbiased form, for the census enumerators and directory compilers had no vested interests as did reformers looking for proof of the evils of drink.

Although we can never know the differences in criminal and noncriminal drinking patterns in Columbus, there are many ways to see how the criminal class differs from the noncriminal classes. The family situations of the criminals, their ages, their birthplaces, occupations, place of residence, and personal property owned can be compared to the general population. These descriptive characteristics of the individuals allow the relationship of the criminals to the larger society to be explored, illuminating both similarities and differences between the two, and, more important, allowing the question of whether or not the criminals and noncriminals were in fact two different groups.

Further characteristics of the criminals can be examined. Contemporary sociologists of deviance theorize the stigma of arrest, by which society labels a person as criminal, changes the behavior of individuals.[5] When society treats a person as criminal he becomes criminal, even beginning to internally label himself as "criminal." If this were so in the past, we should expect to see some behavioral changes after people were arrested for the first time.[6]

The types of criminal behavior are so numerous and varied that we might expect different crimes to come from socially distinct groups. Persons committing crimes of violence against others can be predicated to have been different from persons committing crimes without victims, that is, statutory crimes or offenses against morality. And thieves should be different from rapists or those committing assault and battery.

Further, there should be some larger differences between criminals and noncriminals. These differences should come in part from the impact of the large social changes in Columbus during this period as industry and the population grew. The French historian, Louis Chevalier, for instance, explicitly attributes much of crime in Paris during the first part of the nineteenth century to the destruction of cultural roots by migration to the city.[7] And certainly today we hear enough about the "rootless urban culture" to appreciate the theory that migration causes social deviance.

The county court dockets tell us precious little about the defendants—their names, offenses, and, by inference, sex. Were we to use only the dockets for our analysis, there would be little more to do. To remedy this lack of personal information, I used two strategies. First, all defendants who appeared before the court between 1865 and 1875 were searched for in the manuscript U.S. census of 1870, both within the city of Columbus and within Franklin County. Second, for one year on each side of a defendant's court appearance, the Columbus city directories were also searched. Each kind of search had its own advantages and disadvantages. The census, of course, was rich in information, but it was compiled for one year, and many defendants had either left the area or had not arrived yet. The directories, while providing only occupational information and including mainly urban dwellers, were more inclusive as they were compiled yearly and therefore included people who were not around for the census enumeration. The census search identified 387 persons who appeared in the dockets between 1865 and 1875, while the 1860-83 directories yielded another 947. Adjusting the number of crimes for recidivism, 32 percent of the defendants between 1865 and 1875 were found in the census, and an additional 28.8 percent of all criminals between 1860 and 1883 were found in the directories. Another 9 percent can be added to the criminals identified in the census if the duplicated names are counted, which brings the census-finding percentage up to over two fifths. To put these figures in perspective, we may glance ahead to the finding percents for the paupers, the same percentage of whom were found in the city directories, while far fewer were found in the census (10.5 percent of the paupers for the years 1865-75).

For comparative purposes, a stratified random sample of non-criminal Franklin County and Columbus residents was drawn from the 1870 manuscript census. This sample was controlled to be comparable to the characteristics of those criminals identified in the census; thus the same proportions of rural and urban, men and women, and age stratifications were maintained.[8]

Although a substantial number of defendants who had appeared between 1865 and 1875 were geographically stable enough to be counted during June 1870, a little less than three fifths of them were not. This can be explained in several ways. First, a small number of defendants had been imprisoned during the census enumeration. Second, some defendants were mobile in or out of the county. Third, some were nonresidents; fourth, some died; and fifth, some present were never enumerated. Those imprisoned can be accounted for, and estimates of persons lost through mobility can be established by examining the yearly percent found; the unaccounted-for residual defendants logically belong to one of two categories—nonresidents of Franklin County or residents who were not enumerated by the census takers.

Table 17 displays the number and percent of criminal defendants by the year of their arrest. The percent found figure may be taken as an indicator of persistence, which shows, for example, the proportion of persons arrested in 1865 present in the 1870 census. As expected, the closer a person's arrest was to the 1870 enumeration, the greater was their chance of being identified by the census search.

Two hypotheses can be tested using this information. First, we can predict that the stigma of an arrest and court appearance would accelerate the disappearance rate of criminals: in other words, fewer persons arrested before 1870 should be found than those arrested after

Table 17. Criminals found in 1870 census

Criminals	1865	1866	1867	1868	1869	1870	1871	1872	1873	1874	1875
Total defendants (*a*)	196	120	124	104	155	159	104	164	186	186	211
Number in 1870 census (*b*)	36	24	25	28	36	43	29	41	39	30	41
Percent found in 1870 census (*c*)	18	20	20	27	23	27	28	25	21	16	19
Number in prison in 1870 (*d*)	2	6	5	5	10	6					
Adjusted percent found in 1870 census (*e*)a	19	25	25	32	30	31					

aThis is calculated by adding to the number found in the census those who would have persisted had they not been imprisoned. $e = \dfrac{(c \times d) + b}{a}$

1870. Second, we expect to find that criminal defendants were a part of an especially turbulent and moving population, which implies a sharply peaked curve. The first hypothesis is clearly disproved, for the persistance rates tend to be the same on either side of the census enumeration date. For one year, at least, there was no increase in the inferred leaving rates—exactly the opposite of what we predicted.

What this means is that a person who was to be arrested one to three years after the census enumeration had a fairly good chance of being counted. Arrestees were not immediate newcomers to the area but had been around for about one to three years. Criminals were probably no more strangers to the city than were noncriminals; common people and criminals both moved through the city, the only difference being that one group was willing to offend the state.

If the implications from this persistence table are correctly drawn, then some of our current assumptions about the meaning of mobility out of an area may have to be reconsidered. Ever since Stephan Thernstrom's study of Newburyport, *Poverty and Progress*, it has been assumed that for lower class persons to leave an area was a sign of economic failure or even disaster. Although arrest does not constitute a financial disaster, one would think that for people whose incomes were marginal to begin with, arrest would have made things even more difficult. Further, arrest is a stigma which could be moved away from, which is not necessarily true for impoverishment. Yet our mobility indication shows just the opposite, the disaster of arrest led to stability, or perhaps stagnation, not mobility.

There is an alternative interpretation of the persistence table. The depression of 1873-74 caused admission rates of nonresidents to the poorhouse to soar. There is no evidence to show whether or not this influx of nonresidents had any relationship to crime, but it may have been that the low identification rates for 1873 and 1874 were more due to this influx of paupers than to normal patterns of migration. Unfortunately this interpretation is not testable because the indicator of persistence is an aggregate rather than an individual measure.

The second hypothesis, that criminals were part of a turbulent population, is also disproved. While the graph makes clear that criminals do move away, they do not move away nearly as fast as we might expect. Stephan Thernstrom, in *The Other Bostonians*, provides a useful survey of all decadal persistence studies, which shows that throughout the nineteenth century persistence ranged between 40 and 60 percent. But more useful for us, he also finds an annual disappearance rate of just under 20 percent for the first year after someone has appeared.[9] Similarly, Peter Knights found in his study of Boston that about 40 percent of a sample disappeared in five years, which suggests that once a person has stayed in a place more than one year, their propensity to leave drops a bit.[10] If we look at the percent found and the adjusted percent found in Table 17, we see that the inferred disappearance rates closely approximate the figures of Thernstrom and Knights. From this measure then, the criminals appear to have been about as prone to move as the rest of the population— neither especially turbulent nor blocked.

At this point we must entertain an alternative source of uncertainty, the possibility that members of the dangerous class were systematically ignored by the census enumerators and city directory compilers. Recent work on the census indicates this is highly probable.[11] If this is the case, then we have two alternatives: to either assume that the people found in the directories and the census were the more respectable and therefore more countable or to assume that they represented the average members of the dangerous class. Since there is no reason in the evidence to go either way, it makes most sense to assume that although many of the criminals were ignored or skipped or missed by the enumerators, that the enumerators ignored people randomly, and that those we did find represent people who otherwise remain just names in the criminal court docket.

The mean family size of criminals identified in the 1870 census was 4.3, slightly smaller than the size of a comparable Columbus family, 4.65. Although criminal defendants were more often single or from small families, they were not social isolates. The important thing is that they were family persons, with a family size distribution approximating that of the larger society. Had the criminal family size been greatly larger or smaller than the noncriminal family, we might have utilized explanations with theoretical import. But average size families make the linking of criminal behavior and the social situation of the family more difficult. Criminals, by this measure, were "normal."

As with family size, the family position or living situation of the criminal population was very similar to that of a randomly chosen noncriminal population. There are a few minor differences of interest, however. The proportion of offenders who were sons was the same as for the city population, but less than for the rural county population. This means that young men who were criminals lived less often under parental supervision than did rural persons; in a sense, the criminal young men all had a more "urban" family situation. The proportion of male heads of households was the same for criminals and the city population also, while the random sample of the rural population has slightly fewer heads of households. And although fewer of the criminals boarded in families than did comparable members of either the rural or urban population, this difference was made up for by the number of criminals living alone, in boarding houses, or in hotels. All these similarities, which are shown in Table 18 confirm the normality of the family sizes and indicate that at least from the point of view of the family unit, criminals mirrored remarkably the population of the county as a whole.

Although they are not in the largest category, those persons living outside the nuclear family deserve a careful look. Seventeen percent of the criminals found in the census, or 61, lived alone, boarded with a

Table 18. *Family position of criminals and comparable city and county population samples*

Position in family	Criminals (N=358)		City dwellers (N=145)		County dwellers (N=196)	
Son	77	(22%)	29	(20%)	61	(31%)
Mother	8	(2%)	5	(3%)	8	(4%)
Father	201	(5.6%)	78	(54%)	93	(47%)
Daughter	6	(2%)	2	(1%)	7	(4%)
Mother, head of household	3	(1%)	3	(2%)	0	(0)
Boards with family	36	(10%)	20	(14%)	27	(14%)
Alone	9	(2%)	1	(1%)	0	(0)
Hotel	7	(2%)	4	(3%)	0	(0)
Boardinghouse	9	(2%)	3	(2%)	0	(0)

family, or lived in a boarding house or hotel. Fourteen percent of the randomly selected rural people lived outside the nuclear family, while 19 percent of the random urban sample did. But comparatively fewer criminals boarded with families: this meant the single individual who committed a crime was less likely to choose a family to live with than was his noncriminal counterpart. Table 19 shows this in a four-fold table. We must remember this does not apply to all or even most criminals, but for this minority, these results are significant. Criminals to a far greater extent than noncriminals choose living situations where their behavior could not be as closely observed and controlled as when with a family.

This finding at once confirms and confounds a hypothesis: if non-family living had been the norm for most criminals, it would be apparent that we were dealing with Dickensian Fagins. On the other hand, if no criminals were found to be living outside of the umbrella of the family, then the vision of criminals lurking off with their own kind could have been dismissed. We are left with both—a few Dickensian criminals and many "normal" criminals.

What kinds of crimes did these unattached criminals engage in? As Table 20 shows, they did tend to specialize, engaging mainly in theft, with statutory crimes the second biggest choice. More impressively, they avoided crimes of personal violence, a fact that makes their behavior seem more purposeful, rational, and economic. The questions we are unable to answer about this group are the most intriguing: did the sample of twenty represent the tip of an iceberg of classic deviants? After all, a majority of criminals were not found in the census, and we might guess that single individuals could avoid enumeration more easily than those attached to families. Or is this group a valid indicator of the actual proportion—6 percent—of criminals who lived out-

Table 19. *Persons living outside the nuclear family, 1870*
(*Chi-square = 9.93*)

Boards with	Criminal	Noncriminal
Family	36	47
Nonfamily	25	8

Table 20. Type of crime and defendant's family

Offense	Lives in family		Lives alone	
Murder	19	(6.3%)	0	-
Rape	3	(1.0%)	0	-
Assault and battery	88	(29.2%)	1	(5%)
Theft	106	(35.2%)	11	(55%)
Theft by trick	11	(3.7%)	2	(10%)
Gambling	1	(0.3%)	1	(5%)
Liquor violation	21	(7.0%)	1	(5%)
Other statutory offense	52	(17.3%)	4	(20%)
Total	301		20	

side the influence of a nuclear family? Or were these the small elite of professionals who plied their business in Columbus? None of these questions can be even guessed at and we must let the matter stand: most criminals for whom we have information were, in terms of family, similar to the whole population, but there was a small number who deviated from the norm and even seemed to choose income-generating criminal activities.

About 22 percent of the criminals found in the 1870 census were below twenty-one years old. This contrasts startlingly with the ages of modern offenders. Today, one half of all property crime is committed by people under twenty-one, while 30 to 37 percent of the persons arrested for crimes of personal violence are under twenty-one.[12] Evidently criminal offenders have become dramatically younger in the past century. The age distribution of the 1870 criminals paralleled closely that of the whole state of Ohio, if the children under fifteen in the state are omitted from the comparison (see Table 21). The coefficient of determination (R^2) is .78 when criminals and noncriminals over fifteen are compared, and when only those over twenty are compared, the ages become even closer, with the coefficient reaching .87.

Table 21. Age distribution for total population of Ohio, 1880, and criminals, 1865-75

Age group	Percent		Cumulative percent	
	Ohio	Criminals	Ohio	Criminals
Under 5	12.7	0	12.7	0
5-9	12.3	1.1	25.0	1.1
10-14	11.4	4.2	36.4	5.2
15-19	10.4	12.2	46.8	17.3
20-24	10.2	15.5	57.0	32.8
25-29	8.1	12.8	65.1	45.7
30-34	6.7	13.7	71.8	60.5
35-39	6.0	12.3	77.8	72.6
40-44	5.0	8.6	83.8	81.1
45-49	4.2	7.1	88.0	88.1
50-54	3.6	6.5	91.6	94.6
55-59	2.9	2.6	94.5	97.2
60-64	2.4	1.6	96.9	98.7
Over 65	3.1	1.4	100.0	100.0

Source: 9th U.S. Census, *Population.*

The median age for criminals was thirty, while two thirds of the offenders were between the ages of 15 and 39. Thus in comparing age, as well as family, criminals in nineteenth century Ohio were remarkably similar to the general population.

It can be argued that arrests only occur with the inexperienced or incompetent criminals; if this is so, then the age of arrested persons might be taken as the indicator of the beginning points of criminal careers. This interpretation means that today criminal careers are beginning at a much earlier age than a century ago. If, on the other hand, the age of criminal defendants is an indicator of the age of all criminals (even those not caught), the situation is equally interesting, for most certainly our nineteenth century criminals were older than those of today. Perhaps the major factor responsible for this change is the change in job opportunity patterns for young people. For in the 1870s young people had jobs which were for many poor (and even middle class) people an important part of the family's financial support.[13]

Recent criminological thinking asserts that crimes committed by young people almost always occur in the context of the gang, even if arrests do not. Further, it is asserted that these offense patterns are a "phenomenon of urbanization."[14] More significant, it has been found that in industrializing nations proportionally few crimes are committed by young people, and criminologists reason that the young people in industrializing nations make up a needed part of the labor market and are therefore more integrated into the dominant society.[15] Certainly the Columbus, Ohio, evidence tends to support this hypothesis.

But, more to the point, the older age of the nineteenth century criminals suggests that the individual context of their behavior may have been less gratutitous than that of modern teenage crime. It is not so much the nineteenth century saw less juvenile crime, but criminal behavior belonged to the arena of activities open to adults more so than it does now. We all know the situation of the young today—underemployed, worshiped, feared, romanticized, and despised by the larger society. In some ways our youth attitudes and the situation of the young corresponds to that of a whole class of people in the nineteenth century, the dangerous class. Indeed, the literature on the dangerous class reminds us of literature on the young today—both horror and fascination with their sexuality, use of drugs and alcohol, general filthiness, shiftlessness, lack of goal-oriented behavior, and their overall threat, symbolic and real, to the values of the dominant society.[16] The important difference is that today the dangerous class is age specific, while in the nineteenth century it was more related to socioeconomic status and included all ages. As a new word, "ageism," creeps into our vocabulary, we begin to see that its usage parallels what may be an actual change in our social structure, age becoming a means of class and status differentiation.

If the twentieth century is the era of age-determined status, then assuredly the nineteenth was a time of ethnically-based status. When the birthplaces of the criminal defendants are compared with those of the total population of Franklin County, several contrasts emerge (see Table 22). Although these birthplace distributions are roughly parallel, native Ohioans are underrepresented in the criminal dockets, as are German-born. The Irish, the English, and New Yorkers are over-represented. This confirms, albeit slightly, popular contemporary opinion about ethnic differences in crime, while the presence of New Yorkers confirms the vision of New York as a source of sin. The Germans did tend to be law abiding, the Irish and English were more rowdy, and native Ohioans did not become criminal defendants as often as the more mobile migrants from other states. Because these figures and conclusions are relative, we must remember that the Ohio born still constitute over half of the offenders.

Thirty-five percent of the criminal defendants, as opposed to 19 percent of Franklin County's noncriminal residents, were born outside the United States. Almost twice as many criminal defendants were foreign-born as compared to the general population. If place of birth is considered as crude measure of mobility—that is, an Ohio resident born outside the state has obviously moved at least once—then criminals were two times as migratory as the average person. More important than a mobility measure, birthplace does show the complaints of many native-born Americans did have a basis in fact: immigrants were more often criminals than nonimmigrants. But, on the other hand, a person's chances of becoming the victim of crime com-

Table 22. *Birthplaces of criminal and noncriminal Franklin County population (in percent, N = 300)*

Place	Criminal	Noncriminal
Ohio	51.0	67.0
Pennsylvania	4.0	4.0
New York	4.0	2.5
Virginia	3.0	3.0
Germany	6.0	9.0
Ireland	9.0	3.7
Great Britain	4.0	2.0
Canada	0.8	0.6
Total native born	65	81

Source: 9th U.S. Census, *Population.*

mitted by an immigrant rather than by a native-born citizen were only about one in three in Columbus, hardly justification for wholesale condemnation of immigrants.

One might expect that the subject of race as related to crime would arise. But of the criminals identified in the census, fewer than 3 percent were black, while their proportion of the whole population in the county was 4.4 percent. Proportionally, blacks engaged in criminal behavior far less often than whites. Barring a much larger survey of the participation of blacks in nineteenth century criminal activity, one can only draw tentative conclusions about the small number arrested. The lack of black criminal activity may reflect an extremely oppressed condition—an oppression which prevented them from even being "normal" criminals. Not until the twentieth century did black people move into a position similar to the nineteenth century immigrant.

The only indication of a criminal's residence if outside of the city is to be found in the manuscript census, as the city directories only irregularly included those outside Columbus in their surveys. Table 23 shows the residence distributions of the total population and of the criminals found in the 1870 census. When criminals are considered alone, there is an apparent disproportion of rural residents which almost disappears when the villages are subtracted from the non-Columbus residents as the left column shows: if urban is considered to include small villages, then about 52 percent of the criminal defendants were from urban areas. However, even when this figure is com-

Table 23. *Residence distribution of criminals and Franklin County population, 1870 (in percent, N=373)*

Place	Criminals	Total population
City	43.5	49.6
County	56.5	50.4
	100	100
Urban (and rural nonfarm)	52.2	54.4
Rural farm	47.9	45.6
	100	100

pared to the total population for Franklin County criminal defendants were still slightly overrepresented by rural farm people.

There is a possibility that urban residents, especially those prone to commit crimes, were less geographically stable than rural residents; because of this the census search turned up more rural than urban residents. Table 24 shows the percentage of urban and rural criminals found for each year, 1865-75, to test this. More urban residents were found close to the target date of 1870 than five years on either side of it. This means city dwelling criminals were indeed more mobile than rural ones and therefore their incidence in the census was low.

If, for instance, 1868-72 had been the only criminal group searched in the census, the rural to urban ratio would have been reversed, with 58.5 percent of the criminals being urban and 41.5 percent rural. To complicate matters even further, if only those arrested in 1870 had been searched for, more rural than urban residents would have been found—55 to 45 percent. Clearly, the form in which the question of residence is placed determines the answer. As it stands, we can tell more about the mobility of rural compared to urban criminals than about the absolute mobility of city criminals. And, unfortunately, there is no comparative data available to tell if these rural/urban

Table 24. *Year of first arrest by urban/rural residence*

Year	Urban	Rural
1865	13 (6.9%)	23 (13.1%)
1866	14 (7.4%)	10 (5.7%)
1867	9 (4.8%)	14 (8.0%)
1868	15 (7.9%)	13 (7.4%)
1869	22 (11.6%)	13 (7.4%)
1870	18 (9.5%)	22 (12.6%)
1871	18 (9.5%)	11 (6.3%)
1872	27 (14.3%)	12 (6.9%)
1873	17 (9.0%)	22 (12.6%)
1874	13 (6.9%)	17 (9.7%)
1875	23 (12.2%)	18 (10.3%)
Total	189 (100%)	175 (100%)

criminal mobility differences merely reflect differences among all the county's population or if the difference was specific to the "criminal class."

As the situation stands, we can argue that rural criminality appears to have been higher than urban criminality. Hobsbawm and Rude have shown in *Captain Swing* how in an industrializing area the rural farm laborers can account for a great deal of social disruption. The occupational distribution of criminals supports this point of view, as by far the single largest occupational group of criminals was farm laborers. When those who labored on their parents' farms are included, the figure rises, and the addition of farmers—the third largest occupation—brings the figure to 30 percent. This figure at once confirms and confuses any hypotheses we might entertain about the role of farm laborers, as the farmers and farmers' sons are quite socially distinct from the laborers, especially from the point of view of having a stake in society.

Only one of the 66 farm laborers arrested in Franklin County was charged with rioting, quite different from the riotous farm laborers studied by Hobsbawm and Rude. (Unfortunately, the nature of the charge and actual offenses could be indirect, with those charged for theft actually guilty of riot and looting; because the court records did not describe the criminal offense in detail, such niceties cannot be accounted for.) One half were charged with theft, one fourth with assault and battery, and one eighth with statutory crimes. When compared to all criminals found in the census, the farm laborers stand out as being economically motivated—one half of them were arrested for theft, while only 35 percent of all others found in the census faced the same charges. Farm laborers, as we might well expect, avoided the urban crime of theft by trick and committed the same amount of assault and battery and statutory crimes as the rest of the criminal population. Thus this troublesome occupational group engaged in what can be considered the basic crimes—fighting and stealing.

Personal wealth is an important aspect of any individual's socioeconomic status, and criminals are no exception. The manuscript census for 1870 lists both the real and personal property value for each household enumerated. For the purposes of this study these two categories have been added together and then categorized into nine separate classifications which indicate the economic standing of the family or household unit. When a criminal was identified in the census the value scoring was for that of the family unit: for example, the financial worth of a man who possessed no property but whose father had $200 of real property and $400 of personal property was coded as $600. Thus the individual valuations are only for the purpose of indicating financial status not for assessing an individual's actual possessions.

Dramatic differences in wealth appear between the urban and rural criminals. Table 25 compares both criminals and the random sample for wealth distribution. Overall the criminals were poorer than the noncriminals: 37 percent had no property, while only 26 percent of the noncriminals had no property. But the urban criminals were poorer than the rural criminals—41 percent and 31 percent respectively had no property, 51 percent and 46 percent had less than $250. Yet this finding's import is modified when noncriminals are brought into the comparison, for urban people were twice as poor as rural people. This means that proportionally more rural poor people became criminals than did their urban poor counterparts. Poverty was more responsible for rural crime than it was for urban crime. In fact, if

Table 25. Real and personal property values, urban and rural criminals (in percent)

Wealth category	Urban		Rural		Both	
	Criminal	Random sample	Criminal	Random sample	Criminal	Random sample
None listed	41	36	31	18	37	26
$ 1-250	10	17	15	9	12	12
$ 251-600	5	3	14	12	10	9
$ 601-1,000	4	3	7	7	6	6
$ 1,001-2,500	16	11	9	14	12	13
$ 2,501-5,000	9	11	9	11	9	11
$ 5,001-10,000	6	5	8	15	7	11
$10,001-26,000	6	4	6	11	6	8
$26,001 and up	2	6	0	3	1	4

$250 is chosen as the cut-off point for poverty, the urban poor were underrepresented in the criminals, the rural poor still highly overrepresented. Had the poor in the city been as criminal as their country cousins, 90 percent of urban crime would have been committed by poor people, not just 50 percent.[17]

There is no evidence to associate urban poverty with crime as there is for rural poverty. Because one half of the people in the city were poor (that is, had less than $250 worth of property), one half of the criminals were poor. This has several implications for the meaning of urbanization and crime, for it illustrates that criminal activity was not the same in the city as in rural areas, where within the dangerous class the poor were in fact often the criminals. From the point of view of personal wealth, the urban context of crime differed greatly from the rural: urban criminals were "normal," not necessarily members of the dangerous class.

Another way to examine socioeconomic status and structure, possibly as important as personal wealth, is by occupation. Table 26 displays the distribution of occupations for those defendants found either in the 1870 manuscript census or in the city directories between 1860 and 1883. Those found in the census are compared to their randomly selected counterparts, an operation which cannot be repeated for the city directories because of lack of information.[18] Even with the measurement difficulties caused by the directories' enumeration of household heads only, some generalizations can be made about the employment pattern of the criminal defendants.

Basically, the job structure of criminals was the same as for noncriminals. It is most surprising that there were not more unskilled criminal defendants, especially when the large proportion of propertyless persons is taken into consideration. Between 24 and 41 percent worked at unskilled jobs, with the city directory showing the lower percentage of persons working in this category. The random sample from the 1870 census shows that this was about the norm for the whole county population. An interpretive problem arises here, for the number of propertyless individuals was greater than that of the whole population: this may mean more than the lack of a relationship between occupation and wealth. It suggests that criminal defendants were persons who had, or claimed to have, occupational status above the increased wealth such status usually implies.

Table 26. Criminal and noncriminal occupational distribution (in percent)[a]

Occupation[a]	Urban		Rural	
	Criminal	Noncriminal	Criminal	Noncriminal
Unskilled	31	34	52	48
Semi-skilled	10	5	5	0
Skilled	31	39	10	15
Proprietors	10	6	21	23
Professionals	5	5	1	3
At home	13	11	10	12

	Urban and Rural		Criminals in directories
	Criminal	Noncriminal	
Unskilled	41	42	23.6
Semi-skilled	8	2	11.4
Skilled	21	25	37.1
Proprietors	15	16	13.2
Professionals	3	4	4.2
At home	12	12	1.1

[a]Rather than list the more than 500 different occupations and the specific coding used for each, I will simply explain my basic approach to the creation of the six categories used in this study. The unskilled category was composed of those who listed their occupations as laborer, those who simply told the enumerator where they worked (for example, "works at brickyard"), and those occupations which required only a bare minimum of training—dishwasher, for instance. The semiskilled category included noncraft occupations such as factory work, jobs which may not have required much more skill than simple day labor but which represented a step up the ladder of pay and regular employment. The skilled category included all craft occupations and the lower white collar jobs such as store clerks and salesmen. Of course, some white collar jobs were coded with the professionals, the Clerk of Court, for instance. Professionals ranged from lawyers to callings such as allopathic physicians and music teachers. Proprietors included all positions which required skills which we associate with entrepreneurial abilities: the ability to manage capital, make decisions, manage labor, and understand the economic system. This category therefore contained a large range of income and social status, from peddlers to farmers to manufacturers. Some might disagree with this categorization (although it would not make too much difference in the analysis of criminals and paupers), but I am firmly convinced that we must not let sheer economic power unduly influence our view of the meaning of

continued

people's occupations. Although the procedure used in this study does not preserve the white collar/blue collar dichotomy, it has value in its inclusion of the rural population (especially farm laborers and farmers, who were coded as unskilled and proprietors respectively) and in its appreciation of what jobs meant to those who held them. This scheme approximates an alienation scale, the unskilled being the most alienated from their labor, the proprietors the least alienated.

Why? Had they slipped from former positions of congruent status and wealth; had they been occupationally mobile but received no rewards; were they simply unable to exploit their occupational positions; was the added income of a skilled occupation still no help for many families in accumulating even a little property; did a relatively high status job lack the economic meaning which we ascribe to it; did the criminals drink up their added earnings?

In any case, the occupations of the criminals are enough to show that we must readjust our vision of the criminal courts of nineteenth century cities as being filled with the down and out—the unemployable, the unsocialized, and the abnormal. For with some important exceptions, nineteenth century criminals were typical of the whole population.

Urban and Rural Criminals

The data on individual criminals allow us to look again at the relationship of crime to industrial and urban growth. This broad area of inquiry can be reformulated into testable hypotheses. The first hypothesis is that persons who committed crimes defined as "urban" in Chapter 2 will be different from those who committed other crimes. And to look at the question the other way around, we shall ask whether urban residents committed crimes different from those of rural residents. Finally, the question of the socioeconomic status of urban versus rural offenders shall be examined, the prediction being that such status will affect rural criminals in a way different from urban criminals.

Within the whole state in 1870 there were three strongly urban crimes as discovered by the analysis in Chapter 2: murder, theft, and statutory offenses. There was one mildly urban crime—theft by trick—and one nonurban crime—assault and battery. By 1880, with the exception of assault and battery, the situation had shifted: only theft by trick and theft were associated with urban areas strongly, murder and statutory crimes less strongly. Theft as an urban crime was not as sharply distinct as the others, for it also was associated with urban hinterlands. Of all crimes, theft by trick was the only one to show a consistent rate increase in Columbus, where it increased especially during the decade of the seventies. Therefore, theft by trick and theft stand out as being the truly "urban" crimes of Columbus, for the declining importance of murder and statutory offenses shows them to be unimportant as emerging urban crime types. And because the rate of theft by trick did not vary in exact parallel with the rate for theft, they will be analyzed separately, assuming that though both may be "urban," they are not the same kind of phenomena.

There are several reasons why urban criminals (that is, persons tried for committing urban crimes, especially theft and theft by trick) should have been different from other criminals. Presumably such persons have adapted more completely to the urban environment, using modes of criminal behavior associated with the city, than other criminals. And more than just adapting, urban criminals might be expected to exhibit a mastery of the urban environment, exploiting the rapidly changing and growing city in an effective manner. Although the kinds of questions we can ask about these criminals are limited by the data available, we should be able to detect what it was in their backgrounds that made them relate to the urban environment so differently from the other criminals.

The first place to look for differences is in the comparative birthplaces of those committing urban crimes and those committing ubiquitous crimes, shown in Table 27. Except for a slight observed bias toward defendants from the British Isles and corresponding underrepresentation of those born in Germany, the defendants for theft paralleled almost exactly all other defendants. Ethnically they were the same as other criminals.

Unfortunately the number of persons identified in the census manuscript who were defendants in the theft by trick category is too small to allow any reliable statistical analysis, but several differences are at least suggested. Defendants who were arrested for theft involving trick show a difference between themselves and all the others—thieves

*Table 27. Birthplace of urban criminals
compared to all criminals, 1865-75*

Birthplace	Theft by trick	Other theft	All other crime
Ohio	4 (33.3%)	68 (58.6%)	131 (56.2%)
Other U.S.	4 (33.3%)	26 (22.4%)	49 (21.0%)
Great Britain	0 (0)	5 (4.3%)	5 (2.1%)
Ireland	2 (16.7%)	13 (11.2%)	24 (10.3%)
Germany	2 (16.7%)	4 (3.4%)	18 (7.7%)
Europe	0 (0)	0 (0)	3 (1.3%)
Canada	0 (0)	0 (0)	3 (1.3%)
Total	12 (100%)	116 (100%)	233 (100%)

and all other criminals. Fewer who stole by trick were native-born Ohioans; more were born in the United States outside Ohio, and in Germany and Ireland. This means that as a group the "trick thieves" had been more mobile. Such a finding confirms the prediction that trick thieves were urban criminals—traditional thieves were the same as the other criminals. These urban "trick thieves" had experienced more geographical mobility; by this measure they were more rootless and more experienced in the ways of the world. Such characterization conforms to our expectations of what constitutes an urban person, so it comes as no surprise to learn that even in the 1870s, con artists tended to be wily and experienced.

Patterns found in the birthplace distributions are buttressed and added to when the occupations of the criminals are examined. Table 28 shows again, the defendants for theft are similar to the rest of the criminals, with some underrepresentation in the semi-skilled workers and overrepresentation of the unskilled. But the defendants for theft by trick fall into the higher status occupational categories, being underrepresented in the unskilled category and overrepresented in the skilled, professional, and proprietor groups. Such theft by trick apparently required those particular skills (such as literacy, legal expertise, or financial expertise) that are associated with higher skill and status.

When the property worth of the defendants is examined, this suggestion is further supported. Table 29 shows that defendants for

*Table 28. Occupational distribution of urban and all
other criminals, census and city
directory identifications*

Charge	No job and at home	Un- skilled	Semi- skilled	Skilled	Propri- etor	Profes- sional	Row total
			Census				
All other	27	93	22	48	37	9	236
	(11.4%)	(39.4%)	(9.3%)	(20.3%)	(15.7%)	(3.8%)	(100%)
Theft	15	53	5	24	15	1	113
	(13.3%)	(46.9%)	(4.4%)	(21.2%)	(13.3%)	(.9%)	(100%)
Theft by trick	1	3	1	4	3	1	13
	(7.7%)	(23.1%)	(7.7%)	(30.8%)	(23.1%)	(7.7%)	(100%)
Total	43	149	28	76	55	11	362
	(11.8%)	(41.2%)	(7.7%)	(21.0%)	(15.2%)	(3.0%)	(100%)
			City directory				

Charge		No job and at home	Un- skilled	Semi- skilled	Skilled	Propri- etor	Profes- sional	Row total
All other	42	6	95	58	158	65	22	446
	(9.5%)	(1.3%)	(21.4%)	(13.0%)	(35.4%)	(14.6%)	(4.9%)	(100%)
Theft	30	2	84	26	107	27	8	284
	(10.5%)	(0.7%)	(29.6%)	(9.2%)	(37.7%)	(9.5%)	(2.8%)	(100%)
Theft by trick	4	1	8	6	28	13	3	63
	(6.4%)	(1.6%)	(12.7%)	(9.5%)	(44.4%)	(20.6%)	(4.8%)	(100%)
Total	76	9	187	90	293	105	33	793
	(9.6%)	(1.1%)	(23.6%)	(11.4%)	(37.0%)	(13.3%)	(4.2%)	(100%)

theft were a good deal poorer than all other criminals—over 50 percent had no property—while all of the other defendants tended to
occupy the upper wealth categories and had more property than the
average criminal. Not only did the theft by trick defendants have
higher status jobs, they were wealthier.

Family size differences between the three groups of criminal defen-

Table 29. Property value of households of urban
criminals and all other defendants (N = 374)

Charge	$0-$250	$251-1000	$1001 +
All other	108 (44%)	42 (17%)	94 (38%)
Theft	73 (62%)	14 (12%)	30 (26%)
Theft by trick	4 (31%)	1 (8%)	8 (62%)

dants also indicate social differences. The nontheft defendants had a median family size of 4.5, the defendants for theft had somewhat smaller families of 4.1, and the theft by trick defendants had considerably smaller families of 3.6. While none of the theft by trick defendants were living at home as sons, 28 percent of the theft defendants and 20 percent of all others were. On the other hand, 90 percent of those arrested for theft by trick were fathers or heads of households, as opposed to 49 percent for the thieves and 59 percent for all others. The high proportion of household heads suggests that for those stealing by deception, the criminal activity was much more a part of a family economic pattern than for the others.

Urban criminals, as defined by their criminal behavior, differ from those committing nonurban crimes, confirming the original hypothesis. Further, persons committing the two different kinds of theft are differentiated by their socioeconomic status, with the poorer taking the more direct forms of theft, the better off and occupationally successful engaging in the more sophisticated forms of theft by deceit and trick.

The second hypothesis holds that rural persons will commit different crimes from urban dwellers; to explore this, we pursue an empirical comparison of crime by residence of criminal. This approach is based upon a larger theoretical distinction than may at first be apparent. Up until this point we have been using rural-urban crime dichotomies based upon correlations of the incidences of various crime types with urbanized areas: for instance, because there was more theft by trick in urban areas, we defined it as an urban crime. But such a definition says nothing about the persons who actually were apprehended for committing the crimes; as suggested before, there was always the logical possibility that the offenders were actually rural residents, come to the city to commit crime. I argue that for the purposes of defining urban crime types the first approach is valid. This second approach of looking at places of residence should be seen as a way of deepening our understanding the urban-rural crime typologies, of discovering if our larger analysis has validity in specific cases.

Table 30 shows the distribution of crime types by residence, with residence divided into all persons living in any kind of community and those living in the countryside. This table shows that more kinds of crime were committed by urban residents than the analysis in Chapter 2 discovered. Theft by trick is very strongly reconfirmed as an urban crime, but the other kinds of theft are shown to be more rural than most crimes, in apparent contradiction to Chapter 2, which found theft to be associated with urban areas both in 1870 and 1880. Further, murder, assault and battery, and statutory offenses are added to the list of urban crimes.

These findings both support and supplement the conclusions of Chapter 2. The diagram in Table 31 presents the crime typologies

Table 30. Percent urban and rural residence by crime type,
Franklin County, 1870 (N = 313)

	Urban percent	Rural percent	Column total
Gambling	100	0	2
Theft by trick	69	31	13
Murder	61	39	18
Assault and battery	58	42	86
Statute	56	44	55
Liquor	46	54	22
Theft	46	54	114
Rape	33	67	3
County population	54.4	45.6	-

Table 31. Alternative urban crime typologies

Urban/industrial areas in Ohio		Urban residence, Franklin County
1870	1880	1865-75
Murder	Trick theft	Trick theft
Theft	Theft	Murder
Statutory crime		Assault and battery
		Statutory crime
(not statistically significant)		
Trick theft	Murder	
	Statutory crime	
(negative association)		
Assault and battery	Assault and battery	

from this chapter and the second chapter. For Columbus, murder and statutory offenses are reaffirmed as being urban crimes committed by residents of urban areas. Theft in Franklin County was a crime of both urban and rural residents, but the analysis of all of Ohio shows that theft was associated with the immediate hinterlands of cities, which accounts for the rural residents near the city being equally represented in the groups of thieves. Theft by trick and deception was not an urban crime in all of Ohio in 1870, but it was by 1880. The crime rates for Columbus showed this offense on the increase throughout the 1870s as the city went through its period of major industrial growth, so the fact that those who committed this crime between 1865 and 1875 were urban residents reaffirms the urban origins of the theft by trick and deception.[19]

The only crime upon which the two analytic approaches do not converge is that of assault and battery. For the whole state, this crime definitely was not urban, but was ubiquitous. Apparently, only in Franklin County was it the offense of especially urban residents, a vestige of the early urban industrial era.

The third hypothesis to be tested on the data relating to individual criminals is that socioeconomic status will affect the kinds of crimes differently for urban and rural residents. This hypothesis is based upon the knowledge that the different kinds of crimes had different social meanings as well as content, and it is based upon the assumption that urbanization affected behavior, here operating as an intervening variable between socioeconomic status and an individual's criminal behavior. To test this hypothesis, a socioeconomic status scale was constructed for each of the criminal categories, divided by urban and rural residence. The scale is based upon an individual's birthplace (native or foreign), wealth (under or over $250 of property), and occupation (below or above skilled).[20] The scale ranges from a possible low status score of zero to a possible high status score of 100, with most actual scores falling in between as Table 32 demonstrates.

Murderers (and rapists, if we wish to count them) are consistently low in status, whether urban or rural residents. This clearly confirms the previous finding that murder is an urban crime, for the status of the individual defendants shows no reason for the higher incidence of murder by urban residents—the social factor of urbanization can be hypothesized as the intervening variable.

Table 32. *Socioeconomic status scale of urban and rural offenders, rank ordered by type of offense*[a]

Urban	Rank	Rural	Rank
Trick theft	67	Liquor	71
Statutory	64	Trick theft	64
Assault and battery	58	Theft	58
Liquor offenses	51	Assault and battery	58
Theft	50	Statutory	57
Murder	48	Murder	48

[a]See Chap. 4, note 20, for an explanation of the scoring method. Rapists scored lower than all others, 33, but there were too few to be meaningful. Urban gamblers had the highest score, 83, but there were no rural gamblers with which to compare them.

Two of the other urban type crimes—theft and statutory offenses—do not have the same status rankings for the urban and rural residents committing these crimes: both are over seven points apart. For these two crimes therefore we must conclude that the intervening variable of urbanization did not account for the variation between the urban and rural commission of the crimes. As opposed to other kinds of criminals, urban thieves and statutory offenders were different from their rural counter-parts.

Finally, theft by trick, like murder, has a similar status ranking for both rural and urban residents: to account for the difference between urban and rural rates of theft by trick, we must look beyond differences in offenders to differences in the social situation.

Therefore, when socioeconomic status is held constant, only murder and theft by trick emerge as crimes which were clearly fostered by the urban setting. Theft and statutory offenses, on the other hand, stand out as crimes committed by different kinds of persons, depending on whether they were urban or rural residents. Assault and battery remains a troublesome category, the status comparisons indicating it was an urban influenced crime, which is in sharp contradiction to the analysis of the whole state.

What do these three hypotheses tell us about crime and urbanization? First, they show convincingly that indiscriminate lumping together of crime and cities in the nineteenth century is a mistake; such a simple association just does not work. But they do show that there were differences between urban and rural crimes attributable to the effects of the urban environment on people's behavior, effects that overrode socioeconomic status. Murderers and persons who stole by deception came from similar status backgrounds, whether they lived in the city or country, but they behaved differently in the city—stealing and killing more often than in the country. On the other hand, many urban offenders differed in background from rural persons arrested for the same crimes. Thieves, statutory offenders, and liquor law violators in the city came from different status groups than did their country counterparts. Though Columbus, a city of a little over 31,000 in 1870, may not have been a breeding place of criminals, as a growing urban place it did affect the criminal behavior of its inhabitants.

Recidivism

Ramsey Clark recently estimated that 80 percent of all serious crime is committed by previous offenders, while other measures show a rearrest rate of almost 50 percent within a two-year span after release from prison or probation. If a career "criminal class" is not the appropriate word, then we should substitute something else to stand for what appears to be a group of persons committing most of the serious crime in the nation. Since this study is about the nineteenth century, an age which was not afraid to label a dangerous class or a "criminal class," we should be able to identify the career criminal class of a growing city. If the mid-twentieth century is any indication, we will find a large class of criminal recidivists.[21]

About one third, 35.2 percent, of all offenses were accounted for by 631 recidivists; in the twenty-five year period under study, 455 persons appeared before the court twice, 176 three or more times. This leaves about two thirds of the offenses to apparent single-time offenders. By twentieth century standards there was little recidivism in Franklin County and less reason than now to speak of a criminal class.

To judge from current recidivism measures, there must have been an increase in recidivism in the past one hundred years. To discover whether or not this trend had begun in the immediate post-Civil War period, the percentage of yearly cases before the court accounted for by recidivists has been graphed in Figure 6.[22] While no steady increase is visible, it does appear that there was a very slight tendency toward an increasing rate of recidivism. Since recidivism was not measured after 1885, a fall-off in the percentage should be expected near the end of the period—a recidivist beginning a career in 1884 might not have been rearrested until 1886, thus evading the survey.

Another, and perhaps better, way to look at recidivism is to examine the number of first offenders who later became repeaters. When examined in this manner, we then employ the concept of criminal career, and we can ask a different question: given that the overall amount of recidivism was on the increase, does this necessarily imply that there were more individual recidivists? Table 33 demonstrates that there were fewer recidivists beginning their careers as time passed. The figure for the last five-year period should be dismissed be-

Figure 6. Percentage of recidivists, three year moving average

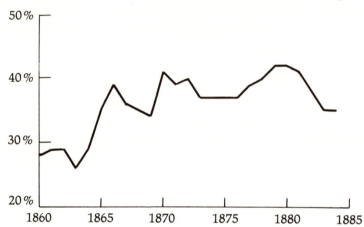

cause no one was traced after 1885, but the other periods show valid percentages. Thus, although the percentage of crimes accounted for by recidivists was on the increase through the whole period, the percentage of persons starting out as recidivists steadily declined.

One of the original hypotheses of this study was that urban and industrial growth would create a career criminal class, and that the origins of this class would be found in the period of industrial and population growth of a city. The evidence indicates this was not the case; in fact, using recidivism starts as a measure of the growth of a class shows just the opposite—urban and industrial growth diminished the number of career criminals.

Table 33. Criminal recidivism: starts of careers, 1859-85

Recidivism	1859-66	1867-71	1872-76	1877-81	1882-85
Crimes by recidivists	380	256	339	269	86[a]
Total crimes	976	710	960	1071	744
Percent by recidivists	39	36	35	25	12[a]

[a]This low number is due, in part, to the lack of tracing of individuals through the post-1885 period.

The second conclusion to be drawn from this evidence leads us to infer that between the late nineteenth century and the mid-twentieth century a career criminal class has been created, or at least greatly enlarged. Comparing recidivism in Columbus (1859-1885) to modern data, we find that recidivism has almost doubled in the past century. Therefore, if the declining frequency of career criminals in nineteenth century Columbus is typical of the rest of the country, then it is clear that some reversal of this process came about between then and now.

The changing ratio of double to multiple recidivism starts confirms the trend away from a criminal class in Franklin County. In the earliest period there were 2.8 double offenders for every multiple offender. This ratio decreased for the 1867-81 period to 1.4, but then rose through 1885 to 2.4, 2.8, and finally 5.7. Proportionately, two-time offenders increased over three-timers after 1871, but both decreased in proportion to the total number of offenses.

Summary

This chapter was an analysis of the characteristics of individual criminal defendants identified in the census and city directories. The defendants were found to be similar to the noncriminal residents of Franklin County, but with some important differences. More Irish, English, and New York State-born persons were criminals than their presence in the population would indicate; conversely, fewer native-born Ohioans and German immigrants were criminals. Even with the disproportionate distribution, over half the criminals were still native Ohioans. Further, rural residents were slightly overrepresented among the defendants. We may either accept this as a reflection of actual criminal behavior, or we may conclude our measure was distorted by the more mobile urban population—urban criminals may have been more likely to move away (and thereby escape census and directory enumerations) than were rural criminals.

Unskilled workers were not overly criminal, for the occupational distributions of the criminals run very close to that of the whole county. Two groups were overrepresented in the court dockets—farm laborers and semi-skilled workers. The apparently normal status the occupations imply is undercut by the defendants' lack of money; they were not as well off as their noncriminal counterparts. The dissonance between wealth and occupation suggests that criminals tended to be in financial straits more than noncriminals of similar occupational status.

The geographical mobility of criminals was not unusually high, nor did the stigma of arrest make them move out of the county at an accelerated rate. Thus any hypothesis which claims that physical dislocation leads to crime must be discounted.

Several hypotheses about urban crime are confirmed. Persons committing the urban type crimes of theft and especially theft by trick were found to differ from other criminals. Those who stole using trick and deception differed from other thieves: they were more likely to have been German or Irish, were wealthier than other criminals, came from higher status occupations, had much smaller families, and were urban residents. The ordinary thieves had lower status jobs, but had birthplaces similar to those of all other offenders.

By determining whether or not the offenders lived in rural or urban areas the crime typology of Chapter 2 was confirmed, showing that murder, theft by trick, and statutory crimes were indeed urban crimes in 1870. Only with one crime, assault and battery, was there disagreement between the individual analysis and the earlier ecological analysis, for in Franklin County, urban residents more than rural residents were arrested for this crime.

The origins of the career criminal class seem to have been more in the pre-Civil War, pregrowth period of the city rather than later. By using the first offense of criminal recidivists as a measure of the growth or decay of a criminal class, it is clear that the criminal class declined as Columbus grew and industrialized. But not only did the class decline, the absolute number of crimes committed by recidivists increased, suggesting that the older criminals stayed in the community and active. This has many implications. For one, the finding that the criminals were not especially different from the noncriminals in their social characteristics hints that the reasons for being criminal were in the society's inability to employ all of its members; thus some occasionally engaged in criminal activities. And once labeled criminal, a person had difficulty reintegrating into noncriminal society. Thus those who became criminal in the pregrowth of Columbus tended to stay criminal. But as the city industrialized and grew, ordinary people were forced less and less to enter the class of criminal recidivists.

One wonders if perhaps the increasing anonymity of a large city population did not interfere with labeling of criminals to a certain extent, making single-time offenders less likely to be rearrested. It would be most instructive if this aspect of the analysis could be followed further, investigating the comparative socioeconomic status of offenders as well as recidivism through the last part of the nineteenth century and early twentieth century. For at some point the process must have reversed, the offenders becoming less like the nonoffender population, the recidivism starts and total amount of recidivism increasing. The question would be to find when and why this change took place—with the rise of the automobile? the end of immigration? with the increasing geographical separation of social classes and suburbanization of the city? with changes in the social mobility process? with the development of modern police information systems?

5 • Paupers in Franklin County, 1867-1881: The Poorhouse

Pauperism, as the word has come to be used in Sociology, is analogous to parasitism in biological science.

Robert Hunter (1904)

Robert Hunter's attitude toward paupers was more sympathetic than the quotation above suggests in that he was one of a small group of people concerned with the problem of poverty. Yet his definition of pauperism as parasitism reveals an underlying assumption, common to many, that paupers took sustenance from society without returning anything of value. More than useless, paupers were drags on social progress; they corresponded, in his organic analogy, not to the diseased parts of a plant, as some modern theorists of deviance would have it, but to the disease itself. One would expect, given such assumptions on the part of those who administered to the parasites, that more attention would have been paid to the disease, rather than the treatment. Yet the great bulk of writings on American poverty in the late nineteenth century, as well as the great bulk of historical writings on poverty today, ignores the paupers themselves, dealing almost exclusively with social welfare institutions.

What should have been important questions went unasked. Were the paupers measurably different from other people? Where did they come from? Were they only certain ethnic groups? Were they all old and sick or young and able? What drove people into pauperism: urban growth, depressions, or simply ineptness? Did paupers move from place to place, searching for some form of better opportunity? Were paupers homeless, or did they claim to have a place called home, some kind of allegiance felt to a community? And how much did the incidence of crime relate to the incidence of pauperism? Did the two forms of "dangerous" behavior respond to the same causal forces, or did they vary independently?

The effects of this ignorance and the corollary assumption that paupers were poor through their own errors and flaws can best be seen in the late nineteenth century dispute over the effects of indoor and outdoor relief: the question of offering aid in institutions or to people in their own homes. From the perspective of the mid-twentieth century such a dispute seems foolish, for we continue to emphasize community aid to the poor, community treatment centers for the mentally ill, and are even beginning to work toward community treatment of criminals. Of course, nineteenth century reformers would have been horrified by these recent trends. By their theory, only the isolation of the defectives and the inculcation of morally and spiritually uplifting values could restore the deviants to health. Thus, while the intellectual energy of social reformers went into this discussion of outdoor versus indoor relief, the poor themselves went ignored.

We, as historians, suffer the effects of this argument. With only a few exceptions both kinds of relief continued to be administered side by side throughout the nineteenth century. We are left with no clue as to whether or not the institutionalized poor were different from those receiving outdoor aid. For this study my assumption has been that while indoor relief and outdoor relief differed in their philosophies of aiding the poor, those receiving the aid were, no matter what their location, from the same dependent class of people. While the late nineteenth century argument against outdoor relief was strong and polemical, no one, as far as I can ascertain, claimed that different kinds of persons were receiving the different kinds of public assistance. Rather, the discussion centered around the allegedly evil effects of outdoor relief, the effects of which were thought to have created and enlarged the dependent class.[1] For these reformers, the reasons to get all the poor into the poorhouse involved two purposes: first to make poverty an unattractive situation, and second, to create an opportunity to reform the poor, making it possible for them to work their way upward. Josephine Lowell, for instance, presented both English and American reports which showed that outdoor aid stimulated poverty. Inverting what seems to be obvious causal priority,

Lowell and other reformers claimed that the increase in public assistance caused both an increase in demand for aid and an increase in the overall number of paupers.

In fact, it seems safe to assume that only the most needy and desperate of the poor came to the poorhouse, the bottom of the bottom of society. The poor who did not come to the Columbus poorhouse but received outdoor assistance were evidently not quite as desperate, and probably there was another strata of poor who never received public assistance. Unfortunately, estimating the relative sizes of these groups is difficult if not impossible. The trustees minutes of the Franklin County Infirmary have some occasional data, which are reproduced in Table 34, but the information raises more questions that it answers. In the monthly figures, were the same people being aided as in the previous month? What was the extent of the aid? For some months, it is unclear whether or not the figures are for individuals or for families. When a family of four got partial support for one month, could we say this was equivalent to one person being in the institution for a month? If dollar expenses were available, perhaps we could estimate this, but as it stands we can only observe that many people dependent on public aid were not in the poorhouse.

Further confusion results from the official dual function of the poorhouses. By the second half of the century, almost every Ohio county had its poorfarm or poorhouse. Usually located within a few miles of the county seat, these institutions were designed to be virtually self-sufficient. In 1850 the institutional names were officially changed by the state legislature to county infirmary. As the title change implies, these institutions had been serving at least two categories—the destitute and the sick. Even the official forms for recording the names of inmates reflected this dual function, where the person's reason for admittance was put in a column titled "disease."

State law required the infirmary director to keep two kinds of record: one a set of minutes of the meetings of the board of directors with lists of income and expenses—the administrative record; and the other a list of persons admitted to the infirmary. It is this second list which is of value to historians interested in history "from the bottom up." For this list constitutes a kind of census of some portions of the bottom segment of nineteenth century society. It is important to con-

Table 34. Indoor versus outdoor relief recipients,
Franklin County, 1860-81[a]

Date	Indoor[b]	Outdoor	
		Families	Individuals
March 1869	-	-	298[c]
September 1873	594	191	524
March 1874	1,132	-	924[c]
September 1875	572	-	1,620
September 1876	762	-	1,652
March 1877	510	620	-
September 1878	675	377	-
October 1878	51	418	-
November 1878	60	472	-
December 1878	57	578	-
January 1879	74	675	-
February 1879	79	671	-
March–September 1879	-	Av. 502/mo.	-
May 1880	33	160	-
June 1880	27	178	-
July 1880	22	152	-
August 1880	55	136	00
September 1880	35	167	00
March–September 1880	-	Av. 323/mo.	-
October 1880	31	236	-
November 1880	58	290	-
December 1880	52	338	-
January 1881	32	301	-

Source: Records of the Business Meetings of the Board of Trustees (1860-72) and Minutes of the Board of the Franklin County Infirmary (1872-82). Indoor relief figures calculated from data.

[a]The outdoor relief figures are assumed to be per month, except for 1873-78.

[b]These figures are the total number of individuals served per year or month, which ever seems appropriate.

[c]Unclear whether or not families or individuals.

ceive of the people included in the list as one group, the financially dependent—not two groups, the sick and the poor. Only the poor sick persons came to the infirmary, illness and pregnancy constituting the same kind of financial disaster for the poor that destitution did. For those people who lived on the margins of pauperism, it did not matter whether the end of a low-paying part-time job or illness precipitated the crisis; the result in any case was the same—application for some kind of public welfare.

For every person who was admitted to the infirmary after 1867 we have a set of remarkably complete records.[2] The manuscript infirmary admittance records include the individual's name, age, residence, birthplace, "disease," admittance and discharge dates, and remarks (which usually related to administrative matters such as billing the person's home township). These records give us a powerful data base from which to study paupers as they fit (or did not fit) into the structure of the larger society. The perspective adopted in this chapter corresponds to that of Chapter 3, with only the official record being used to build up an accurate and detailed set of rates and tables. But because the information is more detailed than the court records, it is also possible to give a general social description of the people who became desperate enough to enter the poorhouse.

The poorhouse data will allow us to test four main hypotheses concerning the effects of urban/industrial growth on poor people. First, if urban/industrial growth caused poverty, then there would have been an increase in the number of persons in the poorhouse who would formerly have been employed. More paupers would have been of working age and there would have been more nonillness admittances. Second, if urban/industrial growth caused mobility and social dislocation, then the poorhouse should have admitted more nonresidents as well as more migrants to the area. Third, if urban/industrial growth created unemployment of a more steady, nonseasonal nature, then the seasonality of the admittance rates of the potentially employable should have decreased. And fourth, if urban/industrial growth caused an increase in poverty, it can be assumed that this occurred through the same social processes as the changes in crime. Poverty rates should have correlated highly with urban and economic crimes.

Poorhouse Inmates

What kinds of people entered the Franklin County Infirmary? An overall description of these people and their usage of the poorhouse is worthwhile for several reasons. First, it will help illuminate our ignorance of the social dimensions of a group which the larger society spent a small amount of money and a large number of words trying to eliminate. Second, we want to know if there was anything except lack of money which distinguished the paupers from the nonpaupers. Third, perhaps we may find that in describing the paupers we will learn some reasons why these people were paupers and what it meant to be a pauper in a medium sized American city in the nineteenth century.

Paupers used the poorhouse according to the dictates of season. This in itself is not too surprising, but a closer examination of monthly admittance patterns graphed in Figure 7 brings out an anomaly. The most severe months of winter weather, the months which provided the fewest job opportunities for construction and farm labor, did not have the highest admittances. Instead, March and November were the heaviest months. We can only speculate about the reasons for this: perhaps the temporary coal and snow shoveling jobs of winter provided more income then we have realized; or perhaps, for those people unable to work, the months of November and March were months of adjustment to the difficulties of winter and spring. As Merle Haggard sings in a recent song about economic hardship: "If we make it through December, Everything's going to be allright, I know."[3]

Figure 7. Poorhouse admittances by month, 1868-81

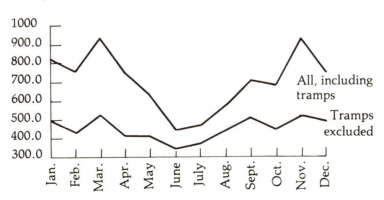

The age structure of the poorhouse population reveals several items of interest. First, the overall poorhouse population was unexpectedly young—ignoring those infants who were born in the poorhouse, the median age was only thirty-one years. But, this population was not as youthful as that of the county from which it was drawn, where 50 percent of the male population (and it is safe to assume about the same for the female population) was 21 or older. This comparison is confirmed by comparing the proportion of the poorhouse population of school age to that of the whole county: about 30 percent of the total Franklin County population was of school age between 1870 and 1880, yet only 10 percent of the poorhouse population fit into this age group.

Table 35 shows the age distribution for all of Ohio, compared with every person who passed through the poorhouse during the period

Table 35. *Age/sex distribution for Ohio, 1880,*
and poorhouse, 1867-81 (in percent)

Age group	Men (N=4,620)		Women (N=1,662)	
	Ohio	Poorhouse	Ohio	Poorhouse
Just born	-	2.9	-	5.8
Under 9	25.1	5.8	24.9	13.8
10-19	21.7	7.2	22.1	14.4
20-29	18.3	23.6	18.4	27.2
30-39	12.6	18.4	12.7	14.6
40-49	9.1	14.8	9.2	9.2
50-59	6.6	12.4	6.4	6.4
Over 60	6.6	14.9	6.3	8.7
	Adults only			
	(N=3,885)		(N=1,064)	
20-29	34.4	28.1	34.7	41.1
30-39	23.7	21.9	24.0	22.1
40-49	17.1	17.6	17.4	13.9
50-59	12.4	14.7	12.1	9.7
Over 60	12.4	17.7	11.9	13.2

Source: 1880 U.S. Census.

under study—the total poorhouse population. Although age distributions were not compiled for the population of just Franklin County in
the census, it is a reasonable assumption that the age distribution for
the whole state, which is available, closely parallels that of the county.
The first notable contrast is that while the state's population evenly
declines in size from the youngest category to the oldest, the poorhouse distribution almost follows a bell-shaped curve. Comparing the
shape of the distributions, the poorhouse contains dramatically more
people in the 20-29 year old age category. This is certainly contrary to
expectations, for the 20-29 age group should have been the most
employable and the most healthy, yet it was the modal age group of
paupers. The picture is clarified somewhat when the age distribution is
recalculated to include only those over twenty as in the bottom part of
Table 35. Here we see that the 20-29 age group was modal for both the
poor and nonpoor population. More to the point, it appears that there
were fewer male paupers in this age category than the proportion of
all males in the larger population would imply, while women were
highly overrepresented. Of course, for women this corresponds most
closely to the child-bearing age, while for men, it indicates that during
the ages of highest employability, they were in fact underrepresented
in the poorhouse.

Contrary to what we might expect of the decades following the
Emancipation Proclamation, blacks were slightly underrepresented in
the poorhouse population. Race was recorded irregularly in the
poorhouse records, but when it was not noted, it is probably correct
to assume that the person was white. Of interest then is the black percentage of the total—4.3 percent—as compared to the county and city
percentages of blacks—an average between 1870 and 1880 of 4.6 percent for the county or 5.8 percent for Columbus in 1880. This can be
read two ways: first, that blacks in the county were slightly less inse-
cure financially or less subject to temporary destitution than whites or,
second, that discrimination discouraged blacks from taking advantage
of the poorhouse. One cannot but suspect the latter was true, though
proof would be difficult.[4]

Almost one half—47 percent—of the paupers were not born in the
United States. This is about three times the percentage of the county
population which was foreign-born—18 percent in 1870 and 16

percent in 1880. As Table 36 shows, compared to the county, the poorhouse served a far more mobile population, only about a fifth of which had been born in the state. Of the ethnic groups, the Irish were the most overrepresented, with the Germans second. While not surprising given the employment difficulties of any ethnic group, this does contradict the popular myth of the respectability and self-sufficiency of the German population of Columbus; they were often poor and destitute, although they were seldom criminal.

The list of "diseases" or reasons for admittance are the most inherently interesting data from the poorhouse records. It should first be noted that close to 50 percent of the cases had no reason for admittance recorded. It is my judgment that these cases were admitted for reasons of poverty, even though occasionally a category for destitution was cited. There is one major reasons to believe so: the vast majority of persons admitted whose residence was listed as "tramp" did not have a disease listed, and when they did, it was often a disease of the road—frozen feet, for example. While 30 percent of the non-tramps had no disease entered, 91 percent of the tramps had no disease. Because the official philosophy of the infirmary was that only those incapable of work should be admitted, and because many of the poor were capable of work, the poorhouse had officially to look the other way when the needy and unemployed applied for assistance. Therefore, we must consider the 49.9 percent of all the cases which did

Table 36. *Birthplaces of pauper and all Franklin County population (in percent)*

Place	Paupers	County
Ohio	22.0	70.0
Pennsylvania	6.3	3.2
New York	4.5	2.2
Virginia	2.9	2.6
Germany	21.8	8.0
Ireland	18.6	3.4
Great Britain	5.2	2.2
Canada	0.6	0.6

Source: 9th and 10th U.S. Census, *Population.*

not have a disease listed as belonging to the category of poor or destitute, bringing the number of cases in the infirmary which had no medical need to over one half.

As previously observed, the poorhouse admittance rate showed definite seasonality. The same is true of the leaving rate, shown in Figure 8, yet strangely the leaving seasons differed from the entering seasons. Springtime—March, April, and May—was by far the most popular time to depart, with November and January running poor seconds. While we will never know absolutely why these departure months were so popular, some conjectures are in order. Most obviously, spring was planting time, and presumably farm laborers could find some employment then. Further, spring is a season when an out-of-doors existence becomes possible, and, of course, temporary employment (for example, construction work) also becomes more available. However, if the spring departures do make sense, then the January and November departures don't. At this point, they are best explained by the high rate of incoming persons who, no doubt, forced out others—in other words, these were high turnover months rather than just high departure months.

Over 50 percent of the population in the poorhouse came from Franklin County, out of which over 80 percent were from the city. This compares with an acutal distribution of 60 percent of the county's population living within the city in 1880. In other words, city dwellers

Figure 8. *Poorhouse departures by month, 1867-81*

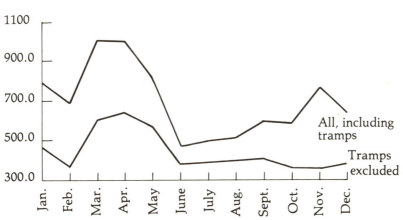

115

were heavily overrepresented in the County Infirmary.[5] We should expect a high degree of accuracy in the reported place of residence for each pauper, because it was in the economic self-interest of the poorhouse to note exactly where each pauper resided, especially within the state. By state law, the township trustees were liable for their own poor, and County Infirmaries could and did collect for their expenses, a time consuming and self-defeating operation.

The other major group of Infirmary inmates were those called tramps. Well over a third of the poorhouse population was composed of "tramps, travellers, or transients." Whether these three different designations were for the same kind of persons is unknown. It is also unknown whether or not all persons categorized as tramps were in fact tramps. My suspicion is that some so-called tramps may have been in fact destitute local people who came to the poorhouse for a meal or two. There are two reasons for this suspicion: first, it probably looked bad for the poorhouse director to allow any employable persons to be given outdoor relief through an institution designed to end outdoor relief.[6] After all, tramps could sleep at the police station.[7] Second, the label tramp avoided the necessity of trying to collect from the person's actual township of residence and allowed a less involved form of treatment—both for the record keeping and the institution itself. And, as discussed in the next chapter, the search to identify individuals in the manuscript census seems to show that at least some of the persons categorized as tramps were, in fact, local residents.

Urban Growth and Poverty

A common assumption about urban industrial growth is that the factory system requires a pool of labor which is underemployed or unemployed and which gives the production system a ready supply of labor whenever needed. This is in contrast to an earlier prefactory era when small-scale production systems bound employer and employed in a less market-responsive relationship which (theoretically) avoided the phenomena of mass unemployment and alienation. If these assumptions are correct, then we should be able to detect a change in the kind and number of persons requiring aid in the Franklin County Infirmary as Columbus went through the transition from an agricultural and governmental service center to a moderately industrialized urban area. Specifically, the ages of persons served should have changed as the more employable were forced to seek public assistance. Table 37 shows the yearly admittance rate to the poorhouse of persons between the ages of 18 and 37, whom I have categorized as the most able-bodied and employable age group in the population.

The first column in the table seems to confirm the hypothesis, for it shows that the trend was toward a higher admittance rate of working age persons throughout the period. The sharp drop in 1881 is probably due to administrative changes within the institution, rather than any external changes. And the economic crisis years of 1872-74 show up clearly with a tripling of admittance rates for this age group.

When the information is disaggregated by sex in the second through

Table 37. *Poorhouse admission rates for 18-37 year olds per 10,000 of Franklin County population (N = 3,447)*

		Men		Women	
Year	Total	Local residence	Non-local	Local residence	Non-local
1867	21.8	3.6	0.0	5.3	0.2
1868	28.3	7.7	3.2	3.2	0.3
1869	26.9	6.9	4.1	3.9	1.3
1870	30.9	12.2	10.3	6.3	0.6
1871	31.3	7.6	7.9	5.1	1.7
1872	45.6	6.7	12.4	6.3	1.0
1873	37.0	4.7	10.6	3.9	0.6
1874	99.7	3.7	33.1	6.5	1.3
1875	30.6	6.8	4.2	4.6	1.1
1876	44.0	5.9	17.3	4.4	0.8
1877	21.9	4.3	4.3	4.9	0.8
1878	39.4	6.8	16.4 ·	6.1	0.6
1879	31.9	6.9	9.8	6.9	1.7
1880	26.8	7.5	8.1	7.3	0.8
1881	18.7	6.1	4.1	5.0	0.4

Source: Estimated annual population from 1860, 1870, 1880, and 1890 U.S. Census.

fifth columns of the table the picture changes and becomes more complex. The trend toward increased numbers of working aged persons no longer holds true for men and women from within the county, as well as those from without, and the time of fluctuations has changed. Admissions for local men actually dropped within the depression of the 1874 period, while 1870 saw a sharp increase of admission rates for them. Local women, on the other hand, follow more closely the overall swings, and were admitted in 1875 with greater than average frequency. Finally, nonlocal men, most often tramps, follow the most curious set of changes. While they account for the bulk of the 1874 increase, it also is clear that they seem to increase biannually—in 1870, 1872, 1874, 1876, and 1878—throughout the decade of the seventies. These men seemed to surge through Columbus at times which probably correspond to geographically shifting labor needs, for example, an increase in employment opportunities in Indiana, as well as to regional or national unemployment.

What then can we conclude from these trends? First, as hypothesized, the pool of working age people serviced by the poorhouse increased throughout the period, which tends to confirm the prediction that the city as it industrialized would require an increased pool of employables. But, second, this pool was not supplied by out-of-work locals, for local men seemed to stay stable in their admission rates, although the proportion of women did increase slightly. Instead, it appears that the class of mobile workers, usually called tramps or transients or travelers by the poorhouse clerks, made up the large proportion of this pool of potential workers. As the city grew, so did the number of poor employable persons, but they were not from Columbus, rather they were migrants or tramps.

Another way of asking if urban industrial growth created poverty is to look at the admission rates divided on the basis of reason for admission to the poorhouse, which was, after all, a hospital too. Table 38 displays the admission rates by year of all those persons with physical or mental ailments as opposed to those who either had no reason for admission or poverty listed.

The trend of admission rates for reasons of poverty rises steadily until 1875, then breaks up irregularly; resulting in a noninterpretable table. And here we see what is often the disadvantage of a disag-

Table 38. Overall sickness and poverty rates per 10,000
Franklin County population for poorhouse (N = 7,342)

Year	Sick	Poor
1867	31.1	33.0
1868	25.6	49.9
1869	21.0	46.2
1870	20.0	54.6
1871	31.6	53.1
1872	32.7	53.2
1873	30.6	55.0
1874	27.8	131.3
1875	29.4	32.8
1876	38.5	59.3
1877	25.7	39.5
1878	32.0	51.4
1879	34.7	44.5
1880	24.1	38.9
1881	21.9	22.1

gregated measure, for only the previous analysis controlling for age confirms the hypothesis, while the crude rate contains much that appears to be "noise."

Current research on urban populations in the nineteenth century indicates that mobility of persons is a central social fact of urban and industrial growth. It is important to ask, therefore, what role the poorhouse played for this mobile population, and for this mobile society. For if it is assumed that a growing urban and industrial area fostered dislocation and mobility, we might reasonably expect that the poorhouse would take in an increasing number of nonresidents, functioning as a cushioning device for the mobile poor. Table 39 displays the per capita admission rates by the place of residence, where these trends can be examined.

Column one shows that the rates for city residents climbed to a peak in 1872 and then dropped back to a fairly level rate. County residents, on the other hand, had two abrupt peaks; one in the late sixties and the other during 1875-76; otherwise, their admission rates also were

Table 39. *Poorhouse admission rates by place of residence
per 10,000 population of Franklin County* (N = 7,786)

Year	City	County	State	Other	Homeless (tramps)
1867	3.8	32.8	1.2	0.3	0.5
1868	22.6	28.0	5.2	4.7	4.9
1869	32.1	11.7	4.6	1.8	8.8
1870	46.0	5.7	0.6	0.2	21.7
1871	48.2	9.0	1.2	0.3	23.6
1872	46.2	6.3	0.6	0.7	27.4
1873	31.3	6.7	0.4	0	31.6
1874	25.7	5.5	0.6	0	113.4
1875	35.6	11.7	0.8	0.1	23.4
1876	35.0	13.7	0.9	0.1	40.3
1877	35.7	7.8	0	0.8	14.2
1878	31.0	7.0	0	0.1	37.3
1879	37.0	8.5	1.0	0.6	25.8
1880	32.5	6.0	0.2	0.2	20.5
1881	22.6	6.9	0	0.1	9.7

stable. With the exception of 1879, state residents made up a decreasing part of the poorhouse population, as did the out-of-state residents. Thus, for persons who claimed a place of residence outside the Franklin County area, mobility through the poorhouse was decreasing. Evidently the proportion of poor who claimed places of residence were diminishing. This apparent trend is contradicted, however, by those poor persons who claimed absolutely no place of residence—tramps. The admission rate of tramps increased from 1867 to a peak in 1875, then dropped back to a rate which never fell as low as the pre-1870 rate.

How does this bear upon the industrial and urban growth of Columbus? Those persons who claimed a place of residence, a sign of a tie to a community, whether local or nonlocal, did not pass through the poorhouse at any increasing rate: but those who had no claimed place of residence did. Therefore, we must conclude that as the city grew, the kind of mobile poor persons changed, with a footloose homeless population claiming an increasing share of poorhouse services.

A person's claimed place of residence is not the only guide to mobility available in the data. It is necessary to look at birthplace also, which indicates whether or not a person has been mobile at some point in the past. Table 40 shows poorhouse admission rates by place of birth, which constitutes a crude mobility measure. If poor people

Table 40. *Poorhouse admission rates controlling for place of birth (in percent, N = 8,315)*[a]

Year	Local[b]	Ohio[b]	United States	Great Britain	Ireland	Germany
1867	0.08	0.07	0.27	1.77	3.42	1.32
1868	0.03	0.10	0.30	2.23	3.41	2.79
1869	0.02	0.09	0.24	2.41	3.04	2.97
1870	0.02	0.14	0.19	3.72	3.12	3.28
1871	0.02	0.18	0.22	3.77	4.33	3.22
1872	0.03	0.20	0.25	4.12	5.74	4.17
1873	0.01	0.19	0.24	4.68	4.59	3.28
1874	0.01	0.26	0.49	14.18	10.96	4.50
1875	0.00	0.19	0.25	2.96	4.17	2.22
1876	0.04	0.26	0.31	4.26	6.86	2.36
1877	0.03	0.27	0.15	2.62	3.61	1.39
1878	0.02	0.19	0.25	4.00	5.79	2.26
1879	0.02	0.30	0.18	2.56	5.07	2.11
1880	0.01	0.25	0.15	3.19	3.48	1.71
1881	0.99	0.17	0.11	1.62	2.65	1.21

Source: 1860, 1870, 1880, 1890 U.S. Censuses.

[a]These rates were computed by dividing the number of entrants with recorded birthplaces by estimated population of the same birthplace within the county. Estimations done by adding 0.1 of the decadal increase for each year. Of course, short-term changes can not be accounted for.

[b]Because of lack of data, the divisor here was simply the total estimated native born.

were migrating to Columbus, where they filled the role of under-employed occasional workers, then we should expect the poorhouse to aid an increasing proportion of these migrants.

Three kinds of trends are visible in the differing birthplaces. These tend to be slightly obscured by the peak of the mid-seventies which affected all but those born in Ohio and Franklin County—a phenomenon, incidentally, which suggests that the bad times of the mid-seventies were more national than local. The three trends visible are a proportional decline of admissions of persons born in Franklin County and the United States outside Ohio; an increasing rate of admissions for native born Ohioans who were migrants to Franklin County and for people born in Great Britain and Ireland; and an apparent increase in the German-born, which began tapering off in the late seventies. This latter trend is of interest, for German migration to Franklin County was just entering its peak, suggesting that either the German community was becoming increasingly supportive and prosperous, or that better-off Germans were moving in. An interesting, though small, contrast emerges between the three groups of native-born Americans, the Franklin County natives and people born outside Ohio entering the poorhouse in decreasing percentages, while the other Ohioans entered the poorhouse on a rising scale. While the data is too skimpy to make large generalizations, we can at least speculate that the ability to avoid the poorhouse for native-born Americans was related to mobility, people who stayed in one place or who moved a long distance avoiding pauperism more successfully than those who moved a short distance within a state.

As Columbus grew and industrialized the turnover or "churning," as historian Peter Knights has termed it, of the poorest elements of the Columbus population shifted from the locally born, German immigrants and U.S. citizens from outside the state, to those from the British Isles. The impoverishment caused by dislocation and mobility were not therefore the universal social effects of Columbus's growth—the effects were disproportionate across different ethnic groups in the population. As a result, by the late seventies and early 1880s a new trend was emerging, with the Irish, the British, and old stock Ohioans appearing to become the newest poor groups. Only those Ohioans who were born and remained in Franklin County decreased their proportion of the paupers; other native-born Ohioans did not fare so well.

Further changes in the nature of poverty rates can be hypothesized to have resulted from changes in the economy and size of Columbus. As observed earlier in this chapter, the poorhouse admittance rates were seasonal, probably responding to an agricultural and construction employment cycle.[8] The important question to ask here is whether or not this seasonality changed: we should expect that for the the poor, working age populace, industrial growth would have decreased the seasonality of poorhouse admittances. However, as the graphs in Figure 9 make clear, no trends over time emerge.

The first graph in Figure 9 shows that relative to the overall poorhouse admittances per year, the potential worker group showed great fluctuations, with a special sensitivity to the depression in 1874. Also, it is of interest that there was an apparent attempt to tighten up admission standards after 1880, resulting in a relative decrease of admissions of the potential workers, an indication that as a group they showed visibly less need than others. The second and third charts are of importance because they display the variation in monthly admittance rates, or seasonality, by year. With range as a measure, 1874 is seen as the year with the greatest seasonality, but when seasonality is charted as a ratio of highest to lowest month, this peak is washed out. This is probably insignificant, as both values rise and fall together, and both show that seasonality followed neither a decreasing nor increasing trend.

Thus, though seasonal admittances to the poorhouse of potential workers were a fact, we can only conclude that the nature of industrial change did not affect this seasonality in any important way. This should not obscure the seasonal variations as an indicator of cyclical fluctuations in the economy. In fact, lack of change in seasonal variation may indicate that those who were actual members of the industrial work force constituted a totally separate group from the paupers and potential paupers, a suggestion which I do not have the data to follow up here.

Urban Crime and Poverty

If poverty, or at least certain kinds of poverty, was fostered by the

Figure 9. Seasonality of working age (18-37), and all poor persons, 1867-81; highest month minus lowest month

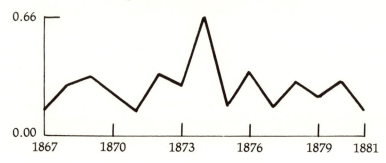

Workers (18-37 year olds) per total admissions

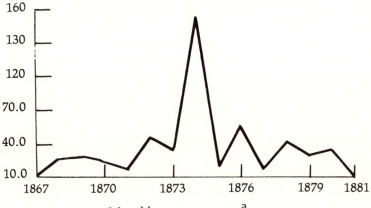

Monthly range per year[a]

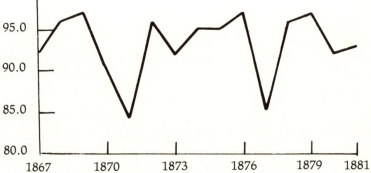

Ratio of monthly admissions lowest to highest

[a]Range is equal to the highest minus the lowest monthly admissions.

growth of the city and of industry, then it should be related to those crimes which also were related to urban industrial growth. Such correlating deliberately ignores any actual social mechanisms which caused crime or poverty, operating instead on the assumption that for whatever specific reasons the two will both have been caused by the same social dysfunction.

The conclusions of the second chapter showed that throughout Ohio two kinds of crime—theft and theft by trick—were strongly associated with and occurred more often in urban/industrial areas. We may therefore treat these crimes as an indicator of the social conditions which characterized late nineteenth century Ohio cities. In Table 41, the correlation coefficients of these two crime types, with two components of theft—petty and grand larceny—also presented separately, and the various poverty rates discussed in this chapter are given.

Of all the variables, the poorhouse admission rate for persons born in Ohio has the most meaningful correlations—$R = .63$ with theft and $R = .53$ with theft by trick. The only other positive correlation of such magnitude is for ill nonresidents. This high correlation of Ohio-born persons with the two most urban crimes should be considered with the previously mentioned increase in mobility of the Ohio-born through the poorhouse. While we cannot infer that the Ohio-born were in fact the urban thieves, we can infer that the conditions which made them more mobile must have been related to the conditions which fostered urban crime.

What then is to be made of this odd relationship between poor, Ohio-born migrants and urban crime? Why do persons born elsewhere correlate negatively or not at all with urban crime? If the place of birth had been recorded with more accuracy, we could ask whether these Ohioans were from rural or urban areas, but only 72 out of almost 1,800 Ohio-born persons listed a city rather than just Ohio as place of birth. Thus the question of urban versus rural origins, rather than state of birth, cannot be answered using the poorhouse data alone.

The one statistically significant relationship between migrants and crime, as well as the absence of other relationships, does not allow us to fallaciously claim that certain kinds of migrants actually committed

Table 41. *Pearson's R for urban crime and poverty rates for Franklin County, 1867-81*

Category	Petty larceny		Grand larceny		All theft		Trick theft	
	R	sig.ᵃ	R	sig.	R	sig.	R	sig.
City resident	.11	(.351)	-.06	(.413)	.07	(.404)	.15	(.290)
County resident	-.31	(.130)	-.39	(.075)	-.38	(.080)	-.42	(.060)
State resident	-.60	(.009)	-.53	(.022)	-.60	(.009)	-.56	(.015)
Out-of-state resident	-.56	(.016)	-.31	(.132)	-.48	(.035)	-.35	(.101)
Tramp	.38	(.080)	.24	(.200)	-.17	(.273)	-.02	(.469)
Working age	.28	(.160)	.16	(.280)	-.02	(.477)	-.17	(.274)
Local worker, men	-.10	(.361)	-.45	(.048)	-.25	(.183)	-.06	(.421)
Nonlocal men	.34	(.108)	.19	(.250)	.13	(.327)	-.06	(.418)
Local worker, women	.26	(.171)	.08	(.394)	.20	(.242)	.33	(.115)
Nonlocal women	.00	(.497)	-.21	(.233)	-.01	(.486)	.08	(.394)
All sick	.27	(.162)	-.04	(.439)	.18	(.264)	.13	(.319)
All poor	.13	(.327)	.00	(.498)	-.14	(.311)	-.34	(.107)
Local birth	-.27	(.168)	-.34	(.106)	-.36	(.097)	-.53	(.021)
Ohio birth	.60	(.010)	.39	(.075)	.63	(.006)	.53	(.021)
U.S. birth	.19	(.249)	.01	(.484)	-.09	(.380)	-.33	(.116)

continued

Category	Petty larceny R	sig.[a]	Grand larceny R	sig.	All theft R	sig.	Trick theft R	sig.
Irish	.30	(.143)	.16	(.279)	.07	(.404)	-.13	(.324)
British	.27	(.162)	.18	(.261)	.03	(.462)	-.17	(.277)
German	-.19	(.248)	-.27	(.168)	-.52	(.023)	-.53	(.021)
European	.28	(.160)	.28	(.153)	.05	(.428)	-.09	(.375)
Sick resident	.15	(.296)	-.13	(.318)	.09	(.369)	.14	(.307)
Sick nonresident	.48	(.037)	.20	(.232)	.59	(.010)	.54	(.018)
Poor resident	-.54	(.019)	-.69	(.003)	-.59	(.010)	-.55	(.017)
Poor nonresident	.36	(.097)	.23	(.208)	.13	(.322)	-.06	(.414)

[a]Sig. stands for significance level, a measure of the chances of an R occurring randomly. .01 is considered the very largest admissible level of significance.

urban and economic crimes, but it does allow some insights into the meaning of migration and urban growth. First, the data about the birthplace show that criminals were more likely to be migrants than noncriminals. We may observe then, that some migrants coped with social change by engaging in criminal behavior. On the other hand, even more migrants failed to cope with social change in such an active and positive way as turning to crime; they ended up financially dependent, in the poorhouse. Lest we conclude that both kinds of reactions were basically similar responses to the new urban environment, the correlations of Table 41 demonstrate that *only* those migrants born outside Franklin County, but within the state of Ohio, became impoverished at the same time as urban and economic crimes increased. The typical paupers were not responding to the same social pressures that the criminals were. Apparently, the social processes leading to impoverishment and crime were very different, as different as the various kinds of criminals and paupers.

Further questions pose themselves. Did the in-state migrants represent a geographically mobile but socially immobile and frustrated segment of society? And were the poor migrants from a greater distance less apt to become members of the dangerous class because their initial motives and social situations were success oriented? Perhaps they had moved because they wanted to, not because they had to. Were they the temporary poor who would strive and succeed? Or perhaps Columbus attracted different, more dangerous, migrants from within the Ohio urban system—a kind of recognition of Columbus's growing urban and criminal status within the regional urban hierarchy. Maybe Minister Washington Gladden's claim in 1887 that Columbus had become the "shelter and safe refuge" for gamblers from other Ohio cities had a larger meaning than he intended, for the city may have functioned as an emerging urban place for the poor criminals from other parts of the state.[9]

Summary

The Franklin County Infirmary, as it was officially known, served both the ill and the healthy, but all were paupers. A survival rate of less than 87 percent assured that those sick persons who could avoid the institution would. Over one half of the people served by the infirmary were probably not sick, but entered for reasons of poverty. The population of the infirmary, even though it served partly as a rest home for old persons, was young, with one half of the population under thirty-one. Even though the infirmary was for all of Franklin County, 80 percent of all the local people it served were from the city—about 40 percent of all the people served. And one third of those served were classified as tramps, with no place of residence. Finally, the poorhouse served more people in winter than in the summer, although the very middle of the winter had a slight drop in admittances. This seasonal variation was increased during the bad times of 1874 when admissions soared. Local residents did not account for these increases, however, for their admission rates stayed stable right through the depression.

Poorhouse admission trends confirm two hypotheses about urban-industrial change in Columbus and fail to confirm two others.

First, admittance rates for working age people who were not from the area increased slightly as opposed to the local workers who showed a stable rate through the period. But when the admission rates of just the poor, not the sick, are examined, no clear trends emerge. Therefore, industrial/urban growth did increase, but only slightly, certain kinds of poverty.

Second, the number of homeless poor increased, while those who claimed homes decreased. Mobility of the poor, as measured by birthplace, changed, decreasing for persons born within the county and for citizens born outside Ohio. The German-born went to a peak in the mid-seventies, then began to decline, though emigration increased. It increased for the Ohio-born outside of Franklin County, for the Irish, and for those born in England, Scotland, and Wales. Therefore, industrial/urban growth increased mobility and dislocation for changing groups of persons.

Third, while seasonality of admittances varied for working age persons, it did not show an overall increase or decrease. Therefore, industrial/urban growth did not affect the seasonality of poverty rates for the employable.

Fourth, poor rates did not, in general, correlate with the economic or urban crime rates. The one important exception was the admittance rate of persons born in Ohio but outside Franklin County. This group has statistically significant correlations with all theft, with petty larceny, and with the crime which has been found to be most highly urban—theft by trick.

We must conclude that the urban and industrial changes which Columbus went through in this period affected the nature of poverty, but not nearly as dramatically as predicted. Certainly, the city's growth caused new kinds of economic distress, but it appears that this distress was more a burden for newcomers to the city than for the older residents.

6 • Paupers

Poverty nests in the cities . . .
    Washington Gladden (1892)

Washington Gladden, though an upper-class Columbus minister, was not afraid to confront the social issue of poverty, even going so far as to tour the slums of New York and London. Yet it took him over twenty-five years to find out that the poor of Columbus lived in misery not unlike the poor of more famous slums, and Gladden never learned of the poverty in the small towns and rural areas outside Columbus. And about the poor people themselves, he knew little if anything. In many ways historians are in a better position for learning than Gladden, because by coupling the various record sets, we can make ourselves a window on the poor of Columbus, whether they lived in downtown alleys or in shacks in the county.

Three questions about Columbus's paupers will be asked here, the answer to be sought in city directories, the manuscript census, and the poorhouse records. How many paupers were there in Columbus and environs? What kind of people were they? And what was the relationship between the paupers, the poorhouse, and the larger society? These questions are all related and are designed to give both an analytic and a general view of poverty as well as some understanding of how the poor were treated by the nonpoor.

Past and contemporary theory assumes that the poor, like Fitzgerald's rich, are "different." The poor are thought to have large (too large) families, often broken families, and no occupations. They relate to the dominant society, if at all, on the edges of the social and physical structures. In post-Civil War America, conventional wisdom held that anyone who really wanted to could achieve financial success, and therefore the unsuccessful were either flawed or lazy. By the end of the century, the intellectuals, if not the more middle-class folk, had moved from blaming the individuals to social Darwinism, which neatly rationalized an evolutionary scheme in which the unfit were nudged out of the mainstream of society.[1] In both cases, the crucial result is that the poor were not considered brothers and sisters of the members of the dominant society, but were of a different social species. Robert Dugdale's famous study *The Jukes* (1877), for instance, isolated an extended kinship network of deviants and defectives, his attitude and approach reminding one of a study of some subspecies.[2] This kind of attitude allowed the "concerned" citizens of Columbus to not see the poor, to deem it necessary to travel to England or at least New York to see some genuine poverty.

The very high rate of mobility of the poor, ranging from the tramps who stayed in town overnight to those who established a place of residence for a year or so, encouraged a kind of social facelessness. And because the poor were not such an agressive social threat as the criminals, they could be allowed to stay shifting and faceless without excessively worrying the dominant society. The major record keeping institution which dealt with the poor in Franklin County was the infirmary, an institution with the ostensible purpose of reintegrating individuals into society, a purpose belied by its actual function of keeping the poor faceless and moving. The route to success in Columbus was not through the poorhouse.

About three times as many persons entered the poorhouse between 1867 and 1881 as there were defendants in the criminal courts during the same period. Yet, only 174 were turned up in the census search, one half as many as the criminals. On the other hand, 29 percent of the paupers, virtually the same percentage as the criminals, were found in the directories. These figures indicate the extremely transient nature of the paupers compared to the criminals. When yearly enumerations as in the directories are the search basis, similar percentages are found, but when a decadal record like the census is used, then very few paupers are found.[3] Apparently the paupers were no more residentially mobile than the criminals on an annual basis, but were far more mobile when the basis of examination is increased to five years.

The underenumeration of the census is so great that one doubts that mobility accounts for it all. It all presumably indicates the extremely low degree of social visibility of the paupers, suggesting that the paupers found in the poorhouse records represent an invisible part of Franklin County and Columbus's social order. Even census enumerators were more likely to miss paupers compared to the more visible criminals.

When the paupers found in the census are compared with those not found, these suspicions are further confirmed. Table 42 shows both sets of paupers compared by age groups and by birthplaces. One immediately notices that the paupers found in the census were younger than the paupers not found: almost one half of those found in the census were between 10 and 29, compared to only one third of all the paupers. Even more significant were the differences in birthplaces: those found in the census were overwhelmingly native born, closely conforming to the general population of the county. Within the foreign born, the Irish/German proportions are reversed, compared to the poorhouse, with the Irish in the census heavily outnumbering the German born. These specific differences in birthplace proportions upset a consistent interpretation: the predominance of native born in the census leads to the conclusion that those paupers who were enumer-

Table 42. *Paupers found in census compared to all paupers*
(in percent)

Age	Census paupers	All paupers	Birthplace	Census	All
Just born	–	3.6			
0-9	5.2	7.9	Ohio	60.1	22.0
10-19	16.6	9.1	United States	20.9	31.0
20-29	31.5	24.6	Great Britain	1.2	5.2
30-39	18.2	17.4	Ireland	10.4	18.6
40-49	9.7	13.3	Germany	3.7	21.8
50-59	11.5	10.8	Europe	3.1	0.8
Over 60	7.3	13.3	Canada	0.6	0.6

ated were in fact the "worthy" poor, while the German/Irish differences suggest otherwise. It is probably wisest to base conclusions on gross differences in so small a sample, in this case the native versus foreign born distinction, rather than the lesser differences within the foreign born category, in which case we may say that those paupers who were identified in the census were not representative. They were the "worthy" poor, the visible poor, as opposed to invisible poor who swarmed through the poorhouse. And it is with these biases in mind that we must analyze the sample of paupers found in the manuscript census.

As with the criminals, a slightly disproportionate number of paupers living in rural areas was found. Table 43 compares the population distribution of the whole county, the paupers, and the criminals. The paupers were slightly more rural than the criminals, a finding which strongly reinforces what Chapter 4 suggested, that the city in itself was not a sink of poverty compared to its immediate hinterland.[4] The question this finding raises is not so much why there were so many rural poor, but more, why have we been left with a perception of the big city as the place for poverty? Several reasons seem fairly clear: the poor of London and New York were visible to the whole world, providing the source for thrilling exposés from the early nineteenth century on. No one had heard of obscure places like Hickory Alley in Columbus, Ohio, much less of the tiny villages and farms which dotted the countryside around Columbus. Had the middle-sized urban places provided the model for understanding poverty, we might have inherited a different perception. And even for a city the size of Columbus, the city center and its periphery will always be more visible than scattered places far from the national road or major rail lines.

Geographical mobility out of the area can be established for the

Table 43. Residence distribution of paupers found in census and Franklin County population, 1870 (in percent)

Place	Paupers	(Criminals)	County
Urban	51.0	(52.2)	54.4
Rural	49.0	(47.9)	45.6

paupers by the same method as it was for the criminals. For this purpose, the paupers found in the 1870 census have been categorized by the year when they first appeared in the poorhouse records. Then each of these yearly categories is converted into the percentage of the total yearly poorhouse entries it represents, the expectation being that a bell-shaped curve peaking in the census year of 1870 will be obtained.[5] Yet Table 44 shows that this is not the case. Instead, there is a very slightly declining identification percentage through 1871, after which there is a rise to a peak in 1874, four years after the census enumeration. After this peak there is a sudden fall off to a minute number of cases.

The depression of 1873-74 has had the strongest effect on this oddly shaped curve. The peak in finding percentages for these years is paralleled by the high overall admission rate for the same years, even though the admission rates were slightly lower for residents during the depression. Apparently the depression affected a kind of person who in normal years would not enter the poorhouse, a person who was considerably more stable and socially visible within the community. Though the evidence to differentiate them is not clear, it may be especially true that those who went into the poorhouse during the depression were the persons whom the elite referred to as the worthy poor.

Ignoring the depression peak, the years between 1867 and 1872 need explaining. If these years are considered representative of "normalcy," there is a remarkably low and consistent finding ratio of about four to

Table 44. *Paupers in census, percent of county residents admitted each year*

Paupers	1867	1868	1869	1870	1871	1872	1873	1874	1875
Local residents admitted per year	213	288	262	313	358	266	256	218	246
Number in 1870 census	12	17	11	17	13	24	35	37	5
Percent	5.6	5.9	4.2	5.4	3.6	9.0	13.7	17	2.0

Note: This table should be compared to Table 17.

five percent. Yet the percentages should not be distributed as they are, for they should peak in 1870, not 1872; if the paupers had followed a normally distributed persistence pattern, those in the poorhouse at some point in 1870 were the most likely to have been enumerated in the census. In other words, even if the average length of a poor person's stay in Columbus was one year, we would assume that 20 percent, for instance, would have stayed two years and 10 percent would have stayed three years, creating the expected peak in 1870. Only 1875 looks as it should with few identifications.

Because the peak did not materialize, we must hypothesize three alternative situations. Perhaps, mobility rates among the poor fluctuated wildly and randomly, leaving only an unpredictable residue behind. Alternatively, there may have been a stratum of poor persons who were extremely stable within the community, the 5 percent were the "worthy" poor, and a stratum who were extremely mobile and not visible to the enumerators.

A third alternative is that the experience which ended at the poorhouse affected the mobility rates of individuals, truncating the stay of those who would otherwise have been expected to stay three or four years. The curve of actual persistence may have looked like Figure 10. The model proposed in Figure 10 is supported by the actual percentages found in the census and displayed in Table 44, for what 44 shows is that before their admission to the poorhouse paupers could be found in the census with some success, but afterwards they disappeared. Figure 10 is the inverse of Table 44, and both tell the same tale: poor people, who as a group tended to be geographically mobile to begin with, once they had experienced the disaster which sent them to the poorhouse, rapidly left the area. We have no evidence to suggest specifically why paupers left after spending time in the poorhouse, but it should be noted that the local welfare agencies had a tradition of moving out ("warning out") the financially dependent, a tradition which some unknown mechanism of the poorhouse seems to have kept alive.[6]

If true, this aspect of geographical mobility says more about the nature of the poorhouse experience than any other indicator, for by inference it shows the meaning of entering the poorhouse. By going to the poorhouse, a person signaled that he or she had taken a major step

Figure 10. Hypothetical model of effect of poorhouse admittance on persistence

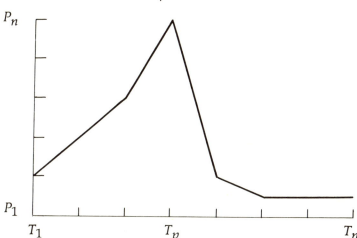

P = Percentage of paupers at any point who remain in an area

T = Time spent living in area

T_p = Poorhouse entry point, which accelerates rate at which paupers leave area

before leaving the area. The experience was a turning point for many; the next move was away from the area. For these people the poorhouse was a transition place, a clearinghouse for the destitute, and not an aid to financial and residential adjustment within the community.

When urban/rural finding rates are divided by year in Table 45, no discernible pattern emerges to explain the high finding rates during the depression years. Nor does a different set of mobility rates appear as it did for the criminals in Chapter 4. The implication is that for the paupers there were no urban/rural mobility differences.

There are two other reasons which might account for the increased identification of paupers after the census year: the amount of property a family possessed and the reason for the individual's admittance to the poorhouse. Both indicate an aspect of status and are factors that can be predicted to contribute to stability. Yet when the reasons for admittance (disease) are broken into two categories—persons admitted for reasons of poverty and persons admitted for all medical

Table 45. *Rural/urban residence by year of poorhouse admission: paupers identified in census*

Year	Rural	Urban
1867	8	4
1868	7	10
1869	6	4
1870	10	7
1871	5	8
1872	10	14
1873	19	16
1874	18	17
1875	2	3
	83	83

reasons, from pregnancy to frozen feet, no differences appear. Sixty-two percent of the paupers found in the census were admitted to the poorhouse for nonmedical reasons, the same proportion as for all the paupers admitted between 1867 and 1881. The distribution of reasons for admittance by year gives no indication of a shift over time which might help explain why more paupers were found among the post-1871 groups. That the years of 1871 and 1872 saw a dip in the number of persons admitted for nonmedical reasons does not conform in any significant way to the finding ratio of Table 44. Depression or not, the precipitants for poorhouse entry stayed remarkably stable.

It might be expected that wealth would explain why more people who entered after 1871 were identified, hypothesizing that they had not yet suffered a financial crisis that would drive them into the poorhouse. However, as with the breakdown by reason for admittance, the answers are disappointing: no clear pattern emerges to link wealth to presence in the census, with the proportion of propertyless persons varying randomly between 1867 and 1875. The only noteworthy feature is the obvious effect of the depression of 1873 and 1874 on those with a moderate amount of property in 1870: more than others, they seem to have been reduced to pauperism. Otherwise, the distribution is inexplicable, as one might expect those with no property in 1870 to be the most numerous category of admittances in 1870, the least numerous on the far sides of 1870.

There is a high correlation between the reason for admittance and property value, as might be expected. Figure 11 graphs this relationship, using the yearly percentage of all admittances for nonmedical reasons and the yearly percentage of those persons who had no property given in the census. With the exception of two years, one of which, 1875, had too few cases to be reliable, the variation is remarkably similar, indicating a strong and predictable relationship between the property value given in the census and poverty as a reason for entering the poorhouse.

Although size of family does not bear directly on the reasons for entering the poorhouse, except in the case of pregnancy, the size and position within the family of the paupers does show something about their social situation. Further, by knowing something about the family, inferences about the effects as well as the causes of impoverishment can be made.

A twentieth century observer probably would have predicted that the families of the poor were larger than the families of the nonpoor, simply as an aspect of cultural differences between the poor and the middle class. Washington Gladden agreed with other observers of the

Figure 11. Paupers in census: no property and nonmedical admittance percents

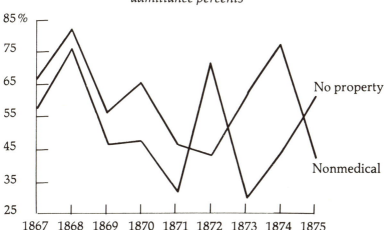

nineteenth century that family size was a *cause* of poverty. "The improvidence which recklessly brings into the world children for whose maintenance there is no provision is one of the sources of poverty."[7]

There were some large pauper families found in the census sample: 10 percent had ten or more members, while over one fourth had seven or more members. But in no way does the evidence support a vision of poor families with swarming armies of children. The mean family size for the paupers found in the census was 4.3; it was very slightly higher, 4.35, for persons admitted for reasons of poverty, and a little lower, 4.22, for persons admitted for medical reasons. This latter difference is accounted for by the large proportion, 18 percent, of single persons admitted for medical reasons. The most impressive thing about the mean pauper family sizes is their similarity to the mean family sizes of the criminals found in the census, 4.3, and the contrast to the random sample taken to compare with the criminals, 4.65.

Gladden was certainly not alone in blaming poverty on improvidently large families; critics from Malthus on had often found that the poor increased their families rather than their individual earning capacities. Yet if the Columbus sample is any evidence, these critics were wrong. At least Gladden was. Here, we must conclude that the elite perception of the poor was determined by ideological assumptions: one assumed the poor were improvident, then looked for ways in which they were improvident. And, of course, some of the poor did have large families, though not larger than their nonpoor counterparts. But because the poor, especially the poor of places like Columbus and its hinterland, were all but invisible, anyone with the common assumptions would selectively perceive only those poor with large families. Or, if an observer did not look for a large family, he could look at a large household, composed of a nuclear family and a boarder, living with another nuclear family. To the elite, all that was visible was a large, faceless "family."

Table 46 shows the distribution of family positions occupied by paupers. The most important figure is for the male heads of households, 34 percent. This means that they were overrepresented in the poorhouse, just as they were in the criminal courts, although to a lesser extent than for criminals where 53 percent were heads of households. With a mean family size of 4.3, there should have been 23 percent in this category; in other words, there were more family men in

Table 46. Family positions of paupers compared to those of criminals and total county population sample

Position in Family	Paupers (N=148)		Criminals (N=358)		Random sample (N=341)	
	Number	Percent	Number	Percent	Number	Percent
Son	24	(16%)	77	(22%)	90	(26%)
Mother	5	(3%)	7	(2%)	13	(4%)
Father	51	(34%)	201	(56%)	171	(50%)
Daughter	10	(7%)	6	(2%)	9	(3%)
Mother, head of household	3	(2%)	3	(1%)	3	(1%)
Boards with family	34	(23%)	36	(10%)	47	(14%)
Alone	5	(3%)	9	(2%)	1	(0)
Child, last name different from family name	5	(3%)	0	(0%)	0	(0)
Hotel	3	(2%)	7	(2%)	4	(1%)
Boarding house	8	(5%)	9	(2%)	3	(1%)

the poorhouse than there should have been. We can only wonder what happened to the families that they too were not in the poorhouse.

The second largest category is of single persons who were living with another family (boarders). There are 9 percent more paupers in this category than in the random census sample, and if those living in hotels and boardinghouses are added, the proportion of boarding paupers goes up to 28.8 percent, twice as many as the random sample. This high proportion of paupers reconfirms the notion of the transience and mobility of the boarding paupers, suggesting that many were workers on the move, taking up temporary living arrangements with other workers. Their solitary situations further indicate an aspect of poverty usually only associated with tramps: impoverishment may have had the opposite context than the creation of large families, may have broken them up, and made even small ones impossible.

Pauper's Occupations

Probably the most startling thing about the occupations of the paupers is that they had any. Yet they did have jobs, at least most of those found in the census and in the directories had. Certainly, we can assume that the paupers called tramps (almost 3,000) did not have regular jobs, although they may have been in transit from one to another. Yet by excluding paupers with residences outside the county from the analysis, over 4,000 county residents are left, almost one third of whom had jobs or at least claimed occupations.[8]

Of course, it is possible that the occupational listings may have been the wishes rather than the actualities of the persons responding to the questions of the city directory compilers. One can imagine the directory compiler banging on the flimsy door of a shack, the wife cracking the door open, the expectant silence of the husband and the family in the dark behind her, and her evasive reply that the head of the household was a laborer. She would not tell the compiler that he was blind and sixty years old, that she had a fever. She would not have known that they would both die in the poorhouse in a few years, leaving no money for their orphaned children.

This is the extreme case of doubtfulness; the other extreme is that the husband really was a laborer, or even a harnessmaker, hard at work while the children were at school and the wife took in some laundry. Reality probably lies in between; my guess, especially in the case of paupers and criminals, is that the occupations they gave to the various enumerators and compilers were the occupations they had when they worked, which may have been very occasionally. Persons listed in the directories without an occupation simply had not been contacted by the compilers, and no neighbor had been able to give the compilers a satisfactory answer. And if a man labored two months out of the year and looked for work the rest of the time, then he gave his occupation as laborer. Stephan Thernstrom points out, for instance, that the most a laborer could expect to work in the 1870s in Massachusetts was 240 days per year; he emphasizes the sporadic nature of work for all unskilled workers.[9] And a survey of 223 workingmen conducted by the Ohio Bureau of Labor Statistics found that they had lost an average of eight weeks of work in 1879.[10] If layoffs were so common among most working people, it would not be unexpected for persons who worked only very occasionally to report that they had an occupation. Occupational distributions, therefore, cannot be used as employment measures, but they can be used as indicators of the occupational structure for poor persons.

If the fact that many paupers had occupations is the most startling finding from the census and directories, the second most startling is that so many had occupations of more status than unskilled workers. One might have guessed that paupers had only unskilled positions, or that, at best, a few of them had semi-skilled positions. Yet Table 47 shows that only between 25 and 40 percent listed their occupations in the unskilled categories. The directories show more persons in the skilled categories than the unskilled and semi-skilled combined. The census, on the other hand, gives a more reasonable proportion of 16 percent skilled, 6 percent semi-skilled, and 40 percent unskilled.

The significance of these findings lies in the doubt they cast on modern assumptions about the status and stability which was inherent in the skilled occupational categories. Thernstrom, when discussing the temporary nature of employment in the nineteenth century, confines himself to "common laborers," referring to them so constantly that one begins to feel they are a separate and very low status group.[11] The occupational classifications for my study were made in the expectations of broad differences emerging from the unskilled versus skilled distinctions. Perhaps, though very real, there were status, in-

Table 47. *Paupers' occupation by reason for admission*

Place found	Unskilled	Semi-skilled	Skilled	Pro-prietors	Profes-sionals	At home
City Directory						
Poor	182	62	254	36	24	106
Sick	110	43	151	22	12	83
Total	292	105	405	58	36	189
Census						
Poor	38	5	17	0	8	20
Sick	33	4	5	0	7	13
Total	71	9	22		15	33

come, and stability distinctions in the nineteenth century which disappeared in the face of impoverishment. A skilled job, moderate income, and small amount of property may not have been enough to preserve a person from the threat of destitution, as it may be today.[12]

Another possibility which might be expected to explain poorhouse admissions for those in other than the lowliest occupational categories is that they were admitted to the poorhouse for medical reasons, for it was a hospital for those who could afford nothing else. The evidence, however, does not support this conjecture. Table 47 shows just the opposite: between 63 and 79 percent of the skilled persons were admitted for nonmedical reasons, higher than average for all admissions. In other words, just because a person had a higher status occupation did not automatically economically distance him from the lower status people who went to the infirmary for reasons of economic need. Though the poorhouse may have served the dregs, they were not all from the bottom of the occupational pile.

When age is brought into consideration, the pattern is made somewhat clearer. In Table 48 we see that almost 70 percent of the unskilled workers were under 30, while only 50 percent of the skilled workers were under thirty. The skilled category is especially interesting, for we see that there appear to be two groups, one under thirty and the other over forty. When the reason for admittance to the poorhouse is added as another variable as in Table 49, it becomes apparent that for the skilled worker, those under forty years old were far more likely to enter the poorhouse for reasons of poverty than those over forty.

Table 48. Number of paupers found in census, by age and occupation

Occupation	Under 20	21-30	31-40	Over 41	Total
Unskilled	19	29	11	12	71
Semi-skilled	3	4	1	1	9
Skilled	2	13	2	11	28
Professional	0	1	3	11	15
Proprietor	1	0	0	0	1
At home	10	10	6	8	34
Total	35	57	23	43	158

Table 49. Number of paupers found in census, reason for admittance to poorhouse, controlling for occupation, by age

Age	Unskilled Poor	Sick	Semi-skilled Poor	Sick	Skilled Poor	Sick	Professional Poor	Sick	Proprietor Poor	Sick	At Home Poor	Sick
Under 20	9	10	2	1	1	1	0	0	0	1	10	2
21-30	19	10	2	2	12	1	1	0	0	0	6	4
31-40	6	5	0	1	2	0	2	1	0	0	1	5
Over 41	4	8	1	0	7	4	5	6	0	0	5	3
Total	38	33	5	4	22	6	8	7	0	1	22	14

For the unskilled workers, a far less consistent pattern is visible, the under 20 and 31-40 groups entering the poorhouse almost equally for reasons of poverty and illness, but the 21-30 year old group entering more for poverty and the over forty more for illness. It seems to me that these patterns are the results of several differing causes: youths with unskilled occupations under twenty years of age were more likely to have the protection of their family in case of economic failure, but once escaping this protection as they grew older, their likelihood of becoming dependent was mainly related to work opportunity, not health. As unskilled workers aged, or, alternately, as older people entered the unskilled category from higher status positions, they would be far more likely to enter the poorhouse because of physical debility; their age and experience presumably serving to keep them financially independent. For the skilled worker, on the other hand, a different set of difficulties was at hand: if the skilled worker was successful, then his economic position kept him from being impoverished by disease, except as he aged and disease took on a more permanent aspect. Thus, the only skilled and young workers who entered the poorhouse were the destitute, victims of either obsolescence or poor economic conditions.

The fact that the risk of entering the poorhouse was almost as great for skilled as unskilled workers should make us question some of the assumptions of modern studies of nineteenth century social mobility. Probably the most widely used measure of occupational mobility is of the step from unskilled to skilled labor. We assume this step was meaningful, yet if it did not even significantly diminish the chances of ending up in the poorhouse at some point, it may have not been as important to the nineteenth century worker as we tend to assume. We need to know much more about the meaning of occupational differences in the lives of individuals before we continue to relate occupation to meaningful social status. We need to add to our own understanding the kinds of disasters nineteenth century working people were close to—not just mortality or mobility, but rapid impoverishment as well. Either that, or we must recognize that being next to the bottom was nearly the same as being on the bottom.

In the decade and a half between 1867 and 1881, there were several changes in the occupational structure represented by the persons entering the poorhouse. Figure 12 gives percentages for the three major laboring categories by year, omitting all others (the unemployed and minor occupations). In all cases an effort was made to find the directory listing closest to the person's admission date. It should not be assumed that the "no job" category is an indicator of unemployment, for it merely indicates missing information.

The relationship graphed in Figure 12 is the most interesting of the occupational changes over the period, for the predominance of the higher status occupations among the poorhouse occupants ended as Columbus industrialized. The semi-skilled and skilled categories have no significant relationship, while the unskilled closely relates to both the semi-skilled ($R = .52$) and the skilled categories ($R = .70$). As the graph makes evident, from 1875 on, the skilled occupational group

Figure 12. *Pauper employment patterns in three major occupational categories*

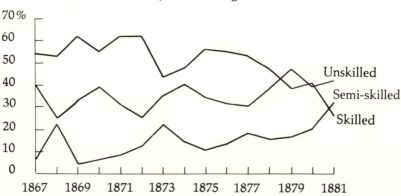

drops, while the unskilled and semi-skilled gain. Thus by 1881 the distribution of occupational categories is closer to what we would expect for paupers, with common laborers and the like making up the bulk of the claimed occupations.

The decade of the seventies, it will be remembered, was a time of both population and industrial growth in Columbus. The industrial growth included increased productivity per worker, which implies that this was a period of technological change as well. As the demands upon the industrial work force grew more sophisticated and rationalized, the employment needs began to resemble the twentieth century situation, where the occupationally advantaged are increasingly rewarded and differentiated from the common unskilled workers. The results were that the poorhouse began to take in fewer skilled workers and more unskilled workers; by 1881 those with skilled occupations were the smallest occupational group of working people entering the poorhouse.

There may have been another component of this occupational shift. In this period of industrial growth, the probability is that workers with craft skills were not suited to the changing demands of growing industry; those who could not adapt found their occupational opportunities shrinking and ended up paupers. Thus the period of change saw some segments of older skilled workers with old skills losing status and falling into poverty, while other workers with the technical skills needed by industry rose in status and security.

Most twentieth century discussions of poverty, or more specifically, welfare, do not focus on recidivism and little contemporary information is available on this problem. We do have the recidivism rates for the Franklin County Infirmary: and if we think of the infirmary as a hospital where local poverty is the disease treated, the recidivism rates provide an indication of cure rates. More important, as with the criminals, the recidivism rates serve as an indication of whether or not the local, chronically impoverished class was increasing or decreasing. Table 50 displays recidivism rates as well as the ratio of double to multiple poorhouse entrants for the period 1867-81.[13]

As with the criminals, the rate of recidivism starts for paupers was decreasing, or the "cure rate" was increasing. Further, the ratio of double to multiple recidivists was also increasing, confirming the trend

Table 50. Pauper recidivism starts, 1867-81

Recidivism	1867-71	1872-76	1877-81
Pauper admissions, recidivists	394	504	330
Total admissions	2294	3720	2802
Percent recidivism	17	14	12
Ratio of double to multiple recidivists	2.5	2.7	3.7

away from multiple visits to the poorhouse. Lest these figures be taken too seriously, we should remember the mobility curve for paupers shown in Table 44. This curve indicated the extreme mobility of the paupers and suggests that pauper recidivism, more than criminal recidivism, needs to be examined over many counties or even states.

It should be reemphasized at this point that a large proportion of the paupers entering the poorhouse had listed occupations in the city directories; the number of persons found in the directories was over one half of the possible linkages. Although the indication is that the paupers were very mobile, at least for a short period of time they seemed to fit into the occupational structure of the city.

Given this information, we can pose two alternative models of the function of the poorhouse in the social structure of the city. The first model is that of the Speenhamland system in the English Poor Law, which earlier in the century had functioned as a supplementary income to the underpaid and underemployed English poor.[14] It is this view of poverty which informs Michael Harrington's description of American poverty before the twentieth century, "When poverty was general in the unskilled work and semi-skilled work force, the poor were all mixed together."[15] This model has the poorhouse taking up the slack in employment opportunities for the various working strata of the city and hinterland, filling in where the business structure left off. It sees the poorhouse as essentially integrative—a preserver of the social order, a wage supplement for a market economy subject to short-term and periodic unemployment.

The other model for the poorhouse, a model which I think is more adequate in its ability to explain both mobility as well as the employment structure of the paupers, is disintegrative. This model sees the poorhouse as taking away from the city those who could not successfully survive in the community, deliberately breaking them from ties to neighborhoods and accelerating them out of the area. This conforms to the colonial practice of expelling or warning out of nonlocal potential paupers, but with a new twist—only those who have tried and failed are warned out.

These two models of the poorhouse's function help explain the issues behind the arguments of late nineteenth century social reformers' dislike of outdoor relief. For outdoor relief was, by its nature, integrative—it aided the poor in their home, neighborhood, and community. Outdoor relief functioned as the English Poor Law, supplementing the inadequate incomes supplied by the local economy. The poorhouse, on the other hand, was a conscious stigmatizing effort, but more than stigma, it aided in breaking up an individual's or family's ties with place, moving the unfortunate out of sight. Washington Gladden's attitude best exemplified the results of this situation, for with all his fame and national reknown as a social reformer, he lived in Columbus over twenty-five years without even realizing where the poor lived. And in his writings, the evils of poverty often seem to mean the evils of the poor whom he cynically parodied as "people who are always looking for work, with both eyes tightly bandaged."[16]

Gladden would have been pleased to know that the county infirmary near him, whether deliberately or not, helped move out the poor, who although they claimed to the directory compilers to have occupations, apparently could not survive in Columbus.

7 • The Dangerous Class

Most if not all the causes of increase of crime are allied to the generic causes—increased density of population, with decreased individual responsibility and increased irritations growing out of, and inseparable from, the complexity of manufacturing and commercial activities.

J. L. Pickard (1885)

Up until this point the question of the relationship of crime and poverty, criminals and paupers in the developing nineteenth century city has not been directly confronted. To do so, it must be realized that there is no simple way to phrase the question in an easily answered form. We of the twentieth century tend to ask whether poverty causes crime, a question which is implicitly environmental in its view of human behavior. Our nineteenth century counterparts, when they bothered, asked about the evils of the dangerous class, their social and ethnic origins, and how they might be successfully kept away from respectable people. Although today we smile at the naivete and frank class biases of the phrase "dangerous class," in many ways it is more serviceable than any with which we have replaced it.

The word class, after all, has two negative connotations: first, it implies the impossibility or difficulty of social mobility, an idea contrary to the American mythos. Second, the use of the word has negative implications for the user, as it reeks of Marxism and at the same time a kind of elitism. So, instead of admitting to ourselves that the poor and criminal might constitute a distinct (and dangerous) class, we talk about third generation welfare families and about criminal repeaters or recidivists. And we know there is a lot of recidivism around.

We have three ways at hand to ask whether poverty caused crime in our test city in the nineteenth century. First, we must agree to let the persons who entered the poorhouse stand for all poor people, the persons who appeared before the county criminal courts to stand for all criminals, and to define the relationship between then in one of three ways. We will first look at the specific persons who were both criminals and paupers during the twenty-five year period under study; second, the socioeconomic differences between paupers and criminals; and third, the relationship between their behavior over time—crime and poverty rates. Each approach has advantages and disadvantages: the first is good in that it doesn't make the ecological fallacy, inferring individual behavior from group characteristics. But it is not so good in its very narrow focus, for surely there were many poor people in Columbus who were never in the poorhouse or were never arrested for a serious offense, yet who were forced by their poverty to steal or earn money illegally. The other two approaches allow generalizations to the larger social system, something difficult with the individual approach. Unfortunately, both of the last two approaches may make the ecological fallacy, attributing to individuals the characteristics of groups.

To find out about persons who were both paupers and criminals, data were created by matching names from the list of paupers and criminals and tallying the matches to provide the scores shown in Table 51. Because the poorhouse data run only from 1867 to 1881, no paupers who became criminals prior to 1867 could be tallied.

Before Table 51 can be analyzed, the question of parameters must be broached: what are the limits above which it may be claimed that poverty caused crime—how many criminals must have been in the poorhouse first? It is this question which requires our subjective judgment, for there are no standards set up or deducible from the original question. If none of the criminals had been paupers or if they had all been paupers the answer would have been easy, but in fact only a few criminals were paupers. We can only conclude that, indeed, some criminals were probably in desperate financial straits, but most had not been reduced to visiting the poorhouse.

Probably the most interesting outcome of tallying paupers and criminals is that almost exactly as many criminals were reduced to poverty by their crime as paupers were driven to crime by their poverty:

Table 51. *Criminals who became paupers and paupers who became criminals, by year*

Category	1859-66	1867-71	1872-76	1877-81	Total
Criminals becoming paupers					
Criminals (once) to paupers (once)	22	15	24	6	67
Criminals (once) to paupers (twice)	3	4	5	4	16
Criminals (twice) to paupers (twice)	17	8	4	1	30
	42	27	33	11	113
Percent of all criminals who were later to become paupers	5.7	5.1	4.4	1.2	3.9

Paupers becoming criminals	1867-71	1872-76	1877-81	Total
Paupers (once) to criminals (once)	25	22	7	54
Paupers (once) to criminals (twice)	4	13	2	19
Paupers (twice) to criminals (once or more)	17	3	3	23
	46	38	12	96
Percent of all criminals who had previously been paupers	8.7	5.1	1.3	3.3

the causation, in other words, ran both ways. This finding more than any other seems to support the nineteenth century vision of a homogeneous dangerous class rather than the twentieth century vision of paupers being driven to crime.

The evidence for the existence of a dangerous class is fairly strong, for there were at least 199 persons between 1859 and 1881 who were both criminals and paupers. These persons were not just misdemeanants and receivers of occasional outdoor relief, but accused felons and poorhouse inmates. This occurred in a county with a total population of 63,000 in 1870; a county where the statistical chance of a person being both a criminal and pauper could account for only one fourth of the actual number.[1]

Further, these numbers are a lower limit, for we must assume that in the late nineteenth century, as today, crimes were unreported; there were few arrests compared to crimes known to the police; and there were even fewer court appearances than arrests. Court records are the tip of a criminal iceberg; this is especially true in this study, for lower courts which tried minor crimes were ignored.

The establishment of a measurable relationship between paupers and criminals makes the discussion of crime and poverty in Columbus more, rather than less, difficult. For by most measures of socioeconomic status, criminals were better off and more residentially stable than paupers. Table 52 compares the criminals, paupers and total county population on the three major measures of status available—birthplace, wealth, and occupation.

What is most interesting in this table is the position of the paupers at the bottom of every scale, with criminals occupying a mid-position between the paupers and the whole society. While there were many propertyless poor people in the county who were neither criminals nor puapers—26 percent had no personal or real property—there were more propertyless criminals, 37 percent, and even more propertyless paupers, 48 percent. The birthplace distributions show a similar rank of status in the Ohio-born category, but not for the other U.S. born and German born. The least agreement for the ranking is in the occupation category—a discrepancy due mainly to the greater proportion of women paupers than criminals.

The large status differences between paupers and criminals, as great as between criminals and the whole population, show that to call criminals and paupers members of a sociologically homogeneous dangerous class is to obscure these important differences. Not only were there socioeconomic status differences between criminals and paupers, but even more significant may have been the much greater rate of geographical mobility, the paupers moving through the county

Table 52. Paupers, criminals, and Franklin County population
(in percent)

Variable	Paupers	Criminals	County
Wealth			
$0	48	37	26
$100-600	20	22	21
Over $650	31	41	53
Birthplace			
Ohio	22	51	67
United States	31	14	15
Germany	22	6	9
Ireland	19	9	4
Great Britain	5	4	2
Canada	0.6	0.8	0.8
Occupation			
Unskilled	40	41	42
Semi-skilled	6	8	2
Skilled	16	21	25
Proprietors	9	15	16
Professionals	0	3	4
At home	29	12	12

Source: Wealth of paupers and criminals is from 1870 census, county from random sample. Birthplace of paupers is from poorhouse records, criminals from census, and population for all of county. Occupation is from 1870 census.

too quickly to be caught in the U.S. census in any numbers to compare with the criminals. Of course, one third of the paupers moved through the county so fast that they were not able to claim a place of residence to the poorhouse clerk; they were recorded as tramps. It is doubtful that there were as many criminals who were tramps, but there is no way of telling.

A partial answer to the question of the relationship of the poor to the criminal may be found through the comparison of rates (done previously in Table 41). In Chapter 5, different kinds of pauper rates were correlated with different crime rates. The most important discovery was the overall absence of statistically significant relationships. One major exception was found in the high correlation between the rates of persons born outside the county but within the state of Ohio with all the different theft rates. We know from the findings of Chapter 4 that 56 percent of all thieves were born in Ohio while 67 percent of all the residents of the county were Ohio born: thus the ecological correlation of poor native-born Ohioans and theft rates must be indicative of undiscovered social changes which affected both geographical mobility within Ohio and theft rates.

Certain differences in the attitudes of persons toward society were probably manifested in the behavior of criminals and paupers, attitudes which parallel their status differences. In status rank, the paupers were less "normal" than the criminals; and their posture toward the dominant society was less normal too, for while the criminals demanded things from society (illegitimately), the paupers were mere supplicants. The action of making a demand corresponds closely to the demands of a "normal" person, the main difference being in the legitimacy of the demands. Paupers, on the other hand, were of such a reduced substratum that they were in no position to make any kind of demand and had to submit their dignity to the county infirmary—they were too "sick" to survive.[2]

Thus the high correlation with theft of Ohio-born pauper rates suggests that when hard times hit the Ohio-born—one of the most socially acceptable groups entering the poorhouse—many natives who were not quite so oppressed by poverty made increasing criminal demands on other Ohio dwellers.

That the criminal action is more aggressive and less alienated than an appeal for aid at the poorhouse adds significance to the fact that the criminals who became paupers slightly outnumbered the paupers who later became criminals. Poverty when defined as pauperism is a lower level of social oppression than is criminality; for those who were downwardly mobile, crime was the step before pauperism; but for those already on the bottom, crime was a step up and not so frequently taken.

When criminals and paupers are seen as vertically differentiated members of the bottom class of society, the question of their relationship changes. Cross-over between the two indicates not a homogeneous dangerous class, but one with subtle gradations and social mobility. But lest we hastily conclude that downward mobility among the bottom groups of society was greater than upward mobility and that this downward mobility was increasing as Table 51 seems to indicate, the "obtrusive" nature of our measures—the criminal court and the poorhouse—must be recalled.[3] The criminal court, especially, is a classic kind of obtrusive measure, as the very appearance of a person before a court constitutes his being labeled a criminal—a label not conducive to future success. As for the labeling importance of the poorhouse, I am uncertain; little in current literature speaks of the stigmatizing effect of that form of welfare. The mobility and very low status of the paupers makes one wonder if the additional label of being a poorhouse pauper may not have made any difference in their treatment by society. But the evidence in Chapter 6 suggests that the poorhouse, too, functioned as a stigmatizing agency.

Even within the criminal group there were status differences, ranging from low status murderers to higher status thieves who stole by deception. There were smaller distinctions within the pauper group as well; although too little is known, it does appear that tramps were at the very bottom.

As important as status differences, and quite likely related to them, were mobility differences between rural and urban dwellers, both paupers and criminals. For although paupers were consistently more geographically mobile than criminals, rural paupers were more stable than urban paupers, and rural criminals were more stable than urban criminals.

Throughout this study, the gross measures of serious offenses and poorhouse admissions have shown mainly differences in kind between urban and rural dangerous classes. On a per capita basis there appears to have been little reason for equating the city with poverty or crime. In fact, the crime and poverty of rural areas, especially the immediate hinterland, seems to be a neglected area of study worthy of careful examination.[4]

But the geographic mobility differences presumably result from an important urban/rural difference. One of the reasons for the growth of Columbus after the war was its advantageous position in the land transportation network; when the canals had provided the heavy haulage system the city's location on a small feeder was a definite disadvantage. But as rail traffic grew in importance, Columbus became an important rail center and crossroads, with the transportation industry becoming a major part of the city's economy. A bird's-eye view map of the city of this period confirms the importance of the railroad, for its switchyards and lines dominate and shape the cityscape. That the urban dangerous class was more mobile than the rural one should be no surprise, for probably the whole urban population was more mobile—certainly the means were available.

We should visualize a five-fold hierarchy to the dangerous class of Franklin County—the rural and the urban, the criminal, the poor, and the tramps. Table 53 provides socioeconomic status scores to support this interpretation.

At the top of the dangerous class were the rural dwelling criminals,

Table 53. Socioeconomic status of criminals and paupers by urban and rural residence, 1870 census (in percent)[a]

Variable	Urban	Rural
Worth		
Criminals	48.0	53.7
Paupers	31.8	45.8
Occupation		
Criminals	57.0	58.6
Paupers	58.8	33.3
Birth		
Criminals	70.0	86.3
Paupers	64.8	88.0
Combined SES scores		
Criminals	57.0	58.6
Paupers	51.8	55.7
County (random sample)	71.0	69.0

[a]See note 21, Chapter 4, for the derivation of this scoring system.

whose status derived from the great number of Ohio-born and the number with farm property. A few of these rural persons committed urban crimes, but those who did so were comparable in social background to the urban dwellers engaging in the same kinds of activity. Overall, rural dwelling criminals had a slightly higher socioeconomic status score than did urban dwellers and were not nearly so geographically mobile. Many were farm laborers. Probably the opportunity or need (unemployment) for moving to another county or state did not occur as often for them as for someone living in an alley by the railroad tracks. No doubt they would not have fared as well in the city as other unskilled laborers; their lack of mobility was a lack of opportunity and alternatives. As a result, these criminals were more responsive to direct economic needs, with the impoverished becoming thieves: the social world of the "criminal element" in the rural hinterland of Columbus was simpler, stabler, and more closed than the city's criminal world.

Below the rural dwelling criminals in socioeconomic status came the urban dwelling criminals, a few of whom were also urban-type criminals. Although there were more urban criminals in the higher status occupations, their foreign birth and lower property worth helped reduce them in status to slightly below the rural dwelling criminals. Urban dwelling criminals moved much more often than their rural counterparts. The stigma of arrest cannot account for this because they had equal mobility before and after arrest, so other, unknown reasons must have been involved. Their social positions were apparently not of enough significance in the community to be affected by the stigma of arrest—at least not enough to make them leave town. This was also true for rural criminals. Only the best off and the worst off were urban-type criminals—the worst off being murderers, the best off being the skilled thieves by deception.

Lower in status than all criminals were the paupers; like criminals, paupers were also divided along rural/urban status differences, the rural ranking much higher than the urban. Although occupationally rural paupers were quite far below urban paupers, this may have been due more to the structure of the rural economy, where most jobs were of an unskilled nature. Otherwise, rural paupers ranked well above urban paupers, the largest difference in any of the four contiguous groups of the dangerous class. Unlike the mobility differences among criminals, both pauper groups had a very high disappearance rate. This suggests that rural paupers had peripheral occupations and only the most tenuous, individualistic relationship to the local farming economy. While rural criminals managed to keep their positions on farms over the seasons, paupers headed for the poorhouse after harvest.

The very bottom of the dangerous class was occupied by two groups: urban paupers, who managed to establish some sort of tenuous residence in the city, and tramps, who in bad times flowed through the city like a river. No socioeconomic status scores for tramps were computed, for without property or occupations, they would have fallen well below all other members of the dangerous class.

According to the socioeconomic status scores, urban dwelling paupers were well below criminals and rural paupers in status, even though for some reason their occupational status was fairly high. Like other paupers, this group did not have much aggression in it, and few became criminals. Though Washington Gladden was wrong in claiming that "poverty nests in the cities," he was correct in perceiving that there were differences in urban paupers, who were much poorer than rural paupers.

It may seem odd to categorize tramps as urban paupers, for by definition they had no place of residence. What makes them urban is the marginal relationship they had to cities in the nineteenth century as now, existing on the outskirts, or in the city wildernesses, both physically and socially. They were also urban because of transportation needs—tramps congregated where trains stopped, roads crossed, and rivers came together. And a willing poorhouse official could provide minimal food and shelter; so probably as a last resort, tramps gave up their social freedom for short periods of time to stay at the Franklin County Infirmary.

Eighty percent of the tramps stayed less than a week; some apparently stayed only for a meal. We have no way of measuring their stay in Columbus outside the poorhouse, but it must also have been brief. Mainly the tramps stayed at the poorhouse during the cold months, with weather and employment keeping them outside in the warm months. Some tramps were found in the 1870 census, a few in the city directory searches. Probably only a tiny fraction of this group ever got enumerated, and we should consider them as a part of the urban poor too mobile to ever pin down, except as they checked into poorhouses.

In many ways the tramps fit the nineteenth century expectations about people in the dangerous class better than the other urban paupers. For one thing, the group was predominantly male, especially those who stayed in the poorhouse during the depression. Further, tramps were younger than other paupers, were almost all white, and were more likely to be foreign-born than other paupers.

The sex composition of tramps is within a half percent of that of the criminals (see Table 54). This suggests that the conventions or social needs which governed the sex composition of the criminals affected tramps in a similar way. A person who tramps, whether out of economic necessity or because he or she was "born wild," has denied community in a physical sense and in a social sense as far as familial

Table 54. Tramps compared to all other paupers (in percent)

Category	Nontramps (N=5,816)	All tramps (N=3,111)	Depression tramps (N=1,021)
Percent female	35.5	7.3	5.6
Median age	34.5	30.5	28.7
Percent black	5.8	1.6	0.6
Percent Ohio-born	26.4	11.4	9.7
Percent U.S.-born	36.8	31.0	32.6
Percent German	18.4	24.1	19.4
Percent Irish	14.7	22.2	23.3
Percent nonmed-ical	37.2	77.6	96.8
Seasonal range[a]	3.4	10.4	20.2

[a]This figure is the result of subtracting the percentage of the total in the lowest month from the percentage of the total in the highest month.

ties and occupational contacts are considered. Their deviance is a threat to the social structure in that the status quo is challenged when visibly different alternative life styles are shown to work. Although the specific threat of crime is not the same as from criminals, the general threat it poses to the social order is. These deviant alternatives were not as open to women as men, just as they were not as open to blacks as whites. While there is little evidence to point either way, we must conclude that the structure of deviant opportunities paralleled the structure of occupational opportunities as far as sexual and racial discrimination. Even the tramp world did not include women and blacks.

The tramp group had a greater percentage of immigrants than did the other pauper groups, but also showed a difference in the small percentage of Ohio-born. Only about 11 percent were born in the state as opposed to over 26 percent of the nontramps. Does this low proportion of Ohio-born mean that the tramps traveled far, ranging well over state borders, or has it no relation to their tramping habits? It is unfortunate that the poorhouse did not record former places of residence of the tramps, for then a crude estimate of their travels might have been made.

About one fourth of all tramps were admitted into the infirmary for medical reasons. Only a tiny percentage of the tramps during the depression were admitted for medical reasons, however. This indicates that there were qualitative as well as quantitative differences between the tramps of the depression and the tramps of more stable times. Just as the tramps of the depression were younger than most tramps, they were healthier—probably they were legitimate victims of unemployment, traveling about the country looking for work and living on public assistance wherever possible. The other tramps were not exactly in the same position, for they were slightly older and a good deal less healthy.

Although both groups of tramps were seasonal in their admittances to the poorhouse, the ones in depression time were the most seasonal. Seasonality indicates the degree of impoverishment suffered by a group, for it demonstrates the group's dependence on seasonal employment and weather. Thus, among the paupers there were three degrees of impoverishment, the tramps of the depression the hardest hit, the nondepression tramps the next hardest, and the nontramping paupers the least hard, two thirds not entering the poorhouse until physical debility pushed them into dependency.

Of all the different groups within the dangerous class the least is known about tramps. Of course, there is some justification for this, but the Franklin County Infirmary records are not unique. The one major work on nineteenth century tramps, *Tramping with Tramps*, by Josiah Flynt Willard, has the virtue of being written from the alleged experience of an upper-class man with a modicum of sympathy for tramps. But Willard's view was biased. When reading *Tramping with Tramps*, one carries away the impression that tramps were tramps because they were lazy and wanted to roam.[5] Further, the tramps mentioned by Flynt seem to have had a median age of about 45, were almost exclusively men, and were mainly native born Americans. Unless the tramps passing through Columbus were atypical, Flynt's account is unbalanced, and one cannot help questioning other aspects of his observations. What we have now is a snapshot of the tramps of Columbus; but many questions about this large and most mobile portion of the dangerous class remain unanswered.[6]

We are left with a picture of the dangerous class of Columbus and its hinterland that is complex and varied. For while differences were found to exist between the rural and urban dangerous class these differences did not emerge as expected. Quantitatively, there was little difference in the amount of urban and rural crime; except for the tramps, there was little quantitative difference between rural and urban poverty. But the kind of people who became members of the dangerous class varied between the city and the country. For although criminals were of higher status than paupers, the rural elements of each group were of higher status than the city dwellers. These differences were probably due to the greater complexity of the urban social structure, where low status persons could exist without becoming official deviants, and also due to the corresponding rigidity of the rural social structure, where criminals were more easily identified and paupers were either economically successful or thrown onto public welfare—there were no alleys to live in near the small farms outside Columbus. And while tramps no doubt scrounged about the countryside near Columbus, the city and the poorhouse were their home for a day.

The city, it appears, did not cause any startling increases in crime or poverty. One wonders how this assertion could ever have been made, for clearly the lowest strata of nineteenth century society were neither noticed nor understood by the larger society. As to those in the dangerous class who never entered the poorhouse or who never came before a court because of a crime, they will remain invisible forever.

How then, should we perceive the social structure of the late nineteenth century city? Until the 1960s the city was looked upon by historians mainly in terms of its literate members. Major concerns were whether or not success was the main goal of Americans, or historians tried to delineate just what image of the city some Americans had held in their minds. When the first studies of the status mobility of city dwellers were begun, a new phenomenon was discovered, that of extremely rapid geographical or residential mobility. This discovery has led us to a rather difficult position: historians now have a substantial body of information but lack theory to explain it. What meaning do we attach to the fact that well over half the residents of a nineteenth century city could be expected to disappear within one decade? This population turnover has made it important for historians to understand in detail the structure of the social systems through which millions of unknown persons moved and acted out their lives. Once we understand the systems, perhaps, we will be able to infer more about the kinds of lives these people led.

When Emerson said, "The past has baked our loaf," he was correct. But it turns out that to understand our loaf, we must learn its ingredients, the baking process, and what kinds of systems produced our bread. Moreover, if we do not like our loaf, we must learn how it has evolved, where its strong and weak points are, and where it is most susceptible to a new kind of yeast. We know that the nineteenth century American cities had a class structure; we know that people seemed to be able to move upward within the middle part of this structure. But we do not know much about the lowest part of this class structure (nor do we really know that much about the upper part).

We are beginning to see that the dramatic process of urbanization which occurred in the nineteenth century may not have affected the class structure as much as we had been inclined to believe. In Columbus, for instance, urbanization did not cause a social disruption which filled the poorhouse and criminal courts with formerly respectable people; rather, it affected the kind and quality of social deviance. Further, it turns out that large parts of the lowest strata of society in the nineteenth century existed in worlds unknown to the rest of society.

Once we achieve deeper insights into all parts of nineteenth century urban society we have more meanings to ferret out. Within just the dangerous class of Columbus, a complex social structure of poor people, tramps, and criminals existed: did this complexity simply result in a highly articulated and confining world for its members, or was it a world of hope, a world where one might wish to move from trampdom to being a petty thief with a more permanent place of residence? Clearly it was a world far removed from that of the literate elite. Lida Rose McCabe in her reminiscences of life in Columbus, portrays a world of stories told by prominent lawyers around parlor tables; a world intimately connected with England and Europe by thought and communication; a world where the Todd Barracks, "wretched hovels of poverty and crime," located just north of the train depot, are remembered more for the governor after whom they had been named than for the members of the dangerous class who occupied them soon after the Civil War.[7]

When we consider the barriers of consciousness and condition that existed between the dangerous class and the rest of society, it becomes apparent that neither of the two alternative modes of interaction—passivity of the paupers or aggression of the criminals—was desirable. Clearly, from the perspective of the dangerous class, aggression was the better choice, a choice made by the more fortunate members of the dangerous class. Our hope might be then, that the children of the people who passed through the poorhouse managed to struggle upward to become criminal offenders, and that their children in turn became integrated into the lower echelons of the occupational structure of society. This wish suggests a separate study, one tracing the careers of the children and grandchildren of the dangerous class. But we should not allow the fate of children and grandchildren to obscure the fundamental inequity of a society which harbors within itself a dangerous class. Nor, because the words "dangerous class" are no longer in vogue, should we be self congratulatory, for the concept delineates the same social reality today that it did a century ago. More current euphemisms conceal the same idea: "welfare families," "subculture of violence," "culture of poverty." The words are new, the problem old, and the solutions still missing.

Notes

1. Introduction

1. See, for instance, Roger Lane, *Policing the City: Boston, 1822-1885* (Cambridge: Harvard University Press, 1967); James F. Richardson, *The New York Police: Colonial Times to 1901* (New York: Oxford University Press, 1970), and *Urban Police in the United States* (Port Washington, N.Y.: Kennikat Press, 1974); Allan Silver, "The Demand for Order in Civil Society: A Review of Some Themes in the History of Urban Crime, Police, and Riot," in David J. Bordua, ed., *The Police: Six Sociological Essays* (New York: Wiley, 1967).

2. Louis Chevalier, *Laboring and Dangerous Classes in Paris during the First Half of the Nineteenth Century,* trans. Frank Jellinek (New York: Howard Fertig, 1973).

3. This is best illustrated by the change in the dollar added by manufacturing value per worker and by the ratio of total population to manufacturing workers, both values computed from the U.S. census for 1860, 1870, 1880, and 1890 for Franklin county.

Year	Dollar added per worker	Manufacturing worker per capita
1860	$ 628.35	.045
1870	673.39	.063
1880	935.63	.066
1890	1204.92	.080

Also, Henry L. Hunker, *Industrial Evolution of Columbus, Ohio* (Columbus: Ohio State University Press, 1958), claims that the 1870s were the turning point in the city's industrial development, but he brings no data to bear on the point.

2. An Ecological Analysis of Ohio

1. Adna F. Weber, *The Growth of Cities in the Nineteenth Century* (New York, 1899), p. 402.

2. Finley Peter Dunne, *Mr. Dooley in Peace and War* (Boston, 1898), p. 125.

3. Charles Loring Brace, *The Dangerous Classes of New York, and Twenty Years Work Among Them* (New York, 1872), p. 47.

4. Robert Hunter, *Poverty* (New York: Macmillan, 1904), p. 198.

5. There are two exceptions: Roger Lane, "Crime and Criminal Statistics in Nineteenth Century Massachusetts," *Journal of Social History*, 2 (1968), 157-163; Waldo L. Cook, "Murders in Massachusetts," *Journal of the American Statistical Association*, 3 (1893), 357-378.

6. Marshall B. Clinard, "The Process of Urbanization and Criminal Behavior," *American Journal of Sociology*, 48 (1942), 202-213. See also his article," A Cross Cultural Replication of the Relation of the Process of Urbanization to Criminal Behavior," *American Sociological Review*, 25 (1960), 255-257.

7. Marshall B. Clinard, *Sociology of Deviant Behavior*, 4th ed. (New York: Holt, Rinehart and Winston, 1974), p. 42. Clinard's observations are based on a book done with Daniel J. Abbott, *Crime in Developing Countries: A Comparative Perspective* (New York: Wiley-Interscience, 1973). For the classic historian's statement, see Arthur M. Schlesinger, *The Rise of the City, 1878-1898* (New York: Macmillan, 1933), p. 114. For more recent studies on urbanization and crime by historians see Michael Feldberg's "Urbanization as a Cause of Violence: Philadelphia as a Test case," and David R. Johnson's "Crime Patterns in Philadelphia, 1840-1870," both of which appear in Allen F. Davis and Mark H. Haller, eds., *The Peoples of Philadelphia: A History of Ethnic Groups and Lower-Class Life, 1790-1940* (Philadelphia: Temple University Press, 1973), pp. 53-70, 89-110.

8. Ernest K. Alix, "The Functional Interdependence of Crime and Community Social Structure," *Journal of Criminal Law, Criminology, and Police Science*, 60 (1969), 332-339.

9. Menachem Amir, "Forcible Rape," *Federal Probation* (1967), XXXI, 56-57. Cited in Marvin Wolfgang, Leonard Savitz, and Norman Johnson, eds., *The Sociology of Crime and Delinquency* (New York: Wiley, 1972), pp. 644-653.

10. See, for instance Clinard, p. 103; Robert H. Bremner, *From the Depths: The Discovery of Poverty in the United States* (New York: New York University Press, 1956), p. 4; Blanche D. Coll, *Perspectives in Public Welfare: A History* (Washington: Government Printing Office, 1969), p. 40. Actually, the implied model of causation seems to be: urbanization caused crime; industrialization caused poverty; but also, industrialization caused urbanization.

11. Brace, p. 225.

12. *Comparison of Ohio to the United States, by agriculture, manufacturing, and population, 1870 and 1880.*

| Category | 1870 | | | |
	U.S.	Ohio	Percent of U.S.	Rank
Large farms[a]	565,054	48,072	8	3
Number of all farms	2,659,985	195,593	7	3
Number of manufacturing establishments	252,148	22,773	9	3
Capital	$2,118,208,769	$141,923,964	7	4
Dollars added by manufacturing	$1,743,898,200	$112,581,913	6.5	
Males employed in manufacturing	1,615,598	119,686	7	4
Total population	28,558,371	2,665,260	6.9	3
	1880			
Large farms[a]	565,054	92,645	5	6
Number of all farms	4,008,907	247,189	6	2
Number of manufacturing establishments	253,852	20,699	8	3
Capital	$2,790,277,606	$188,939,614	7	4
Dollars added by manufacturing	$1,972,755,642	$132,964,132	6.7	
Males employed in manufacturing	2,019,035	152,217	8	4
Total population	50,155,783	3,198,063	6.4	3

Source: Calculated from the *Compendium* of the 10th U.S. Census, 1880.

[a]Large farms were defined as all farms between 100 and 500 acres.

13. Stephan Thernstrom, *Poverty and Progress: Social Mobility in a Nineteenth Century City* (New York: Atheneum, 1970), pp. 139-142.

14. Sherwood Anderson, *Memoirs* (New York: Harcourt, Brace and World, 1942); quoted in Irving Howe, *Sherwood Anderson* (New York: Sloane, 1951), p. 9.

15. Zane L. Miller, *Bos Cox's Cincinnati: Urban Politics in the Progressive Era* (New York: Oxford University Press, 1968), pp. 5,8.

16. SPSS was used throughout this study for data analysis. Varimax rotation was used in this factor analysis. This is a process which creates factors in such a way that each column or factor will have variable loadings near zero or one. This ensures that a variable will clearly be included or excluded from the factors. Underscored loadings are between -1.0 and -0.4 or +0.4 and +1.0 and can be considered the major contributors to each factor.

17. See, for instance, the comment by David J. Armor in his article, "Theta Reliability and Factor Scaling," in Herbert L. Costner, ed., *Sociological Methodology, 1973-1974* (San Francisco: Jossey-Bass, 1974), p. 35.

18. Jerome Hall, *Theft, Law and Society* (Boston: Little, Brown, 1935), pp. 4-132.

19. See Lane, "Crime and Criminal Statistics"; Cook, "Murders"; Theodore M. Ferdinand, "The Criminal Patterns of Boston Since 1849," *American Journal of Sociology*, 73 (1967), 84-99; Elwin H. Powell, "Crime as a Function of Anomie, Buffalo, 1854-1956," *Journal of Criminal Law, Criminology, and Police Science*, 57 (1966), 123-129. (While an important article, Ferdinand's "Politics, the Police, and Arresting Policies in Salem, Massachusetts since the Civil War," *Social Problems*, 19 (1972), 572-588, has too little data for a useful comparison.)

Lane defines serious crimes as those that involve "genuine personal injury or loss" (p. 158).

20. Lane, p. 160.

3. Crime In Franklin County

1. See Richard Quinney, *The Social Reality of Crime* (Boston: Little, Brown, 1970), pp. 16-23, for a classic statement and elaboration of this point of view.

2. Harold Garfinkel, "Conditions of Successful Degradation Ceremonies," *American Journal of Sociology*, 61 (1956), 420-424.

3. A rather unusual serious offense, and one which did not figure in my subsequent analysis, this represents one of the sporadic attempts in Columbus to cut down on general noise, rowdiness, and fun on Sundays. The law reads: "Whoever, being over 14 years of age, engages in sporting, rioting, quarreling, hunting, fishing or shooting, on Sunday, shall . . . be fined not more than 20 dollars, or imprisoned not more than 20 days, or both." Section 7032, *Revised Statutes of the State of Ohio* (Cincinatti, 1884).

4. Thorsten Sellin, "The Significance of Records of Crime," in Marvin Wolfgang, Leonard Savitz, and Norman Johnson, eds., *The Sociology of Crime and Delinquency* (New York: Wiley, 1962), p. 64.

5. The measurement of crime is a very large topic of discussion. See The President's Commission on Law Enforcement and the Administration of Justice, *The Challenge of Crime in a Free Society* (New York: Dutton, 1968), pp. 72-73, for a model of the contemporary criminal justice system. This model's complexity suggests the measurement problems that exist today. Further, the BSSR and the NORC surveys, pp. 98-99, indicate the unreported crimes far exceed the number of reported crimes, which far exceed the number of cases coming to court.

6. As opposed to the recording of the Secretary of State's *Report*, where 16 percent of the offenses were lost by my reclassifications, only 12 percent were eliminated in the county study.

7. See, for instance, Sam Bass Warner, *Crime and Criminal Statistics in Boston* (Cambridge: Harvard University Press, 1934).

8. See Jacob H. Studer, *Columbus, Ohio: Its History, Resources, and Progress* (Columbus, 1873), chap. 6, for a local historian's patriotic version of the Civil War years. England also had crime waves with the ending of wars, low crime during wars. See the article by J. M. Beattie, "The Pattern of Crime in England, 1660-1800," *Past and Present* (February 1974), pp. 93-95.

9.

Average court costs per year

Year	Mean costs	Year	Mean costs
1859	$21.50	1873	$32.10
1860	$24.50	1874	$36.20
1861	$25.00	1875	$35.10
1862	$21.10	1876	$35.30
1863	$37.10	1877	$35.00
1864	$30.00	1878	$35.10
1865	$17.70	1879	$30.20
1866	$23.40	1880	$30.34
1867	$25.40	1881	$31.80
1868	$21.90	1882	$30.60
1869	$26.50	1883	$32.20
1870	$36.00	1884	$28.80
1871	$38.40	1885	$32.40
1872	$33.70		

10. The table below shows total number of arrests by five year period, and makes clear that although embezzlement, fraud, forgery, and obtaining money or goods by false pretenses increased significantly as the city urbanized, they did not rise indefinitely. This suggests that the crime wave was a social event of finite utility, used to establish and then preserve the new behavioral boundaries required for urban life.

Theft by trick for five year intervals, 1860-1899, total arrests

1860-64	1865-69	1870-74	1875-79	1880-84	1885-89	1890-94	1895-99
16	14	37	84	100	152	176	151

11. See Kai Erickson, *Wayward Puritans: A Study in the Sociology of Deviance* (New York: Wiley, 1966), passim.

12. Eric J. Hobsbawn and George Rude, *Captain Swing* (London: Lawrence, 1969).

13. Jerome Hall, *Theft, Law and Society* (Boston: Little, Brown, 1935). As far as the specific crime of being a criminal receiver, there is little evidence to support Hall concerning the difficulty in obtaining convictions. As the two tables below show (by percent) those charged with receiving stolen goods were not greatly different from all criminals, and certainly not in a way we might expect:

Verdicts and pleas for receiving stolen goods, by percent

	Verdict			
Charge	Guilty	Not Guilty	Dismissed	
Receiving stolen goods	12	4	84	$n=49$
All other crimes	17	7	76	$n=2,804$

	Plea		
Charge	Guilty	Not guilty	
Receiving stolen goods	52	48	$n=25$
All other crimes	45	55	$n=1,455$

Criminal receivers tended to be found guilty less than all others, but they also were found not guilty less often. That more were dismissed than average gives some support to Hall, but not with the strength he indicates we should see. Perhaps the defendants perceived that they were on slightly better ground than other defendants because they tended to plead guilty more often than the norm, but this may also mean that they were plea bargaining, feeling a conviction was likely. Thus, although we can gain some insight into the changing social conditions of the city from this crime, we cannot gain much insight into the crime itself from these statistics.

14. Quoted in Jacob H. Dorn, *Washington Gladden: Prophet of the Social Gospel* (Columbus: Ohio State University Press, 1966), p. 311.

15. Cheryl L. O'Brien, "Prostitution in Mid-Nineteenth Century America: A Feminist Perspective" (unpublished paper, University of Minnesota, 1973), has data showing that there were 34 recognized prostitutes and 8 madams in Columbus in 1870.

16.

Verdict	Costs $1-199	$200+	Total
Guilty	435	34	469
Not guilty	1,926	3	1,929
Total	2,361	37	2,398

Chi-square = 124.98

When further broken down this relationship holds as clearly. About 70 percent of the guilty adjudications cost over $50, 70 percent of the not guiltys below $30, and 70 percent of the cases which were laid away cost less than $20. See Eric H. Monkkonen, "Crime and Poverty in a Nineteenth Century City: The 'Dangerous Class' of Columbus, Ohio, 1860-1885" (Ph.D. diss., University of Minnesota, 1973), App. 5, for further detail.

17. *Defendant's sex*

Court costs	Men	Percent	Women	Percent
$1-10	794	25.4	89	36.2
11-20	773	24.7	73	29.7
21-30	487	15.6	33	13.4
31-40	320	19.2	23	9.3
41-50	143	4.6	6	2.4
51-100	412	13.2	18	7.3
101-200	151	4.8	4	1.6
201-500	28	0.9	0	-
501-1,000	11	0.4	0	-
1,000 up	6	0.2	0	-
	3,125	100	246	100

$N=3,371$
Chi Square = 30.4 Significance = .0004

18. See Blake McKelvey, *American Prisons: A Study in American Social History Prior to 1915* (Montclair, N. J.: Patterson Smith, 1972), passim, esp. pp. 130-132, 145.

19. Monkkonen, App. 4, contains graphs of pleas and verdicts by type of offense.

4. Criminals

1. Robert L. Dugdale, *The Jukes: A Study in Crime, Pauperism, Disease and Heredity* (New York: Arno, 1970). See p. 14, for instance, where Dugdale claims that industrialization's lifestyles were ending the bad behavior of the Jukes family.

2. Ely Van De Warker, M.D., "The Relations of Women to Crime," *Popular Science Monthly* (November 1875), p. 1.

3. Charles Loring Brace, *The Dangerous Classes of New York, and Twenty Years' Work among Them* (New York, 1872), pp. 28-29. There is a reasonable objection to raise here. All the rates and interpretations that follow assume that the 16-28 percent of the criminal defendants who were identified in the census manuscript are a reliable indicator of the total population of criminal defendants. They may not have been. Perhaps this approximate one fourth of the criminals were the stable or mobility blocked criminals, while the other three fourths were a totally transient, floating population.

4. *Eighth Annual Report of the Board of State Charities* (Columbus, 1884), p. 20.

5. Probably the best example of labeling theory may be seen in Howard S. Becker, *Outsiders: Studies in the Sociology of Deviance* (New York: Free Press, 1963).

6. On the other hand, if Charles Loring Brace is a typical example, perhaps members of the dominant society labeled so many persons as dangerous that the added label of criminal made no difference whatever in their lives.

7. Louis Chevalier, *Laboring Classes and Dangerous Classes in Paris during the First Half of the Nineteenth Century*, trans. by Frank Jellinek (New York: Howard Fertig, 1973). Ironically, contemporary observers were as likely to see urban mobility as a disruption of the criminal classes and as a disrupter of both criminal activity and the effects of heredity. See Brace, pp. 47-50.

8. Specifically, the sample was drawn as follows. Using a random number table, two sets of random numbers were generated, the total being 387, and divided between city and county in the same proportion as the criminals. The range for each set corresponded to the total number of pages in the manuscript, city and county. Before reordering the random numbers from lowest to highest, each was assigned a value indicating the sex and age (which was categorized by four year intervals) of the person to be sampled. Each random number referred to a page in the census, and the searcher alternatively moved up or down from the center point of the page until a person matching the age and sex assigned to the number was encountered.

9. Stephan Thernstrom, *The Other Bostonians: Poverty and Progress in the American Metropolis, 1880-1970* (Cambridge: Harvard University Press, 1973), pp. 222-225, 308.

10. Peter Knights, *The Plain People of Boston, 1830-1860: A Study in City Growth* (New York: Oxford University Press, 1971), p. 59.

11. See Knights, pp. 144-147, for a discussion of underenumeration. He has four categories of nonenumerated people, but criminals would be likely to only fit in one, that for persons who moved during enumeration.

12. Ramsey Clark, *Crime in America: Observations on Its Nature, Causes, Prevention and Control* (New York: Simon and Schuster, 1970), pp. 54-55.

13. See John Modell and Tamara K. Hareven, "Urbanization and the Malleable Household: An Examination of Boarding and Lodging in American Families," *Journal of Marriage and the Family* (August 1973), table 2, p. 475.

14. Marshall B. Clinard, *The Sociology of Deviant Behavior*, 4th ed. (New York: Holt, Rinehart and Winston, 1974), p. 276.

15. Marshall B. Clinard and Daniel J. Abbott, *Crime in Developing Countries: A Comparative Perspective* (New York: Wiley-Interscience, 1973), chap. 7.

16. See Edgar Z. Friedenberg, *The Vanishing Adolescent* (Boston: Beacon Press, 1959), for the classic discussion of this problem.

17. There is, of course, the possibility that those persons who were arrested in the period 1865-70 had had their financial status altered considerably after arrest. Because our source of information on wealth is of necessity limited to one moment in time we cannot sort out such possibilities.

18. The two tables do not compare exactly for several reasons. First, although the census search did not turn up as large a total number of persons because of geographical mobility, it was more representative, for it included nonhousehold heads—women and children—who were often not found in the city directories. Second, almost everyone in the census was listed with an occupation, while the directories had many omissions. Which one was a more accurate reflection of reality is impossible to determine. And finally, the city directories often listed place of employment, rather than type of work done, which may have introduced unknown and unmeasurable biases.

If the random census sample holds true for the city directory, then we must conclude that the city directory undercounted unskilled workers; or that individuals and the dangerous class in particular exaggerated their occupational status; or that the more complete census included those unskilled persons who were not household heads and did not get into the directories. The city directory and census are in near agreement on the number of defendants in the semiskilled category, 8-11.4 percent, a figure which is higher than the random sample. There is disagreement between directory and census on the number in the skilled group, the census finding 21 percent and the directory 37 percent. This confirms the suggestion that the city directory excluded persons in the unskilled category in favor of the more skilled. Finally, both census and directory agree on the percentage of proprietors—13-15 percent—and the percentage of professionals—3-4 percent.

19. But inferences about crime rates must not be made from these findings, as only the residence of defendants has been established—the crime may not have been committed in the defendant's neighborhood, nor do we have any indication of the defendant's residence at the time the crime was committed. More persons accused of assault and battery, liquor, and statutory violations were identified than the proportions of offenses in each category would warrant. Conversely, proportionally fewer persons accused of murder and both kinds of theft were found.

20. The score was computed in this manner. Each variable, birth, wealth, and occupation, was dichotomized and given a value of 1 for low status and 2 for high status. All foreign-born scores for birth were 1, all others 2. Unskilled and semiskilled occupations were scored as 1, everything else but "at home" and "no job," which were omitted, was scored as 2. Then for each category (for example, residence, birth, and occupation) the average score was

computed and the average for each of the three categories—birth, wealth, and occupation—was then computed. The scores then had 1 subtracted and were multiplied by one hundred for easier comparability.

21. Clark, p. 55; President's Commission on Law Enforcement and Administration of Justice, *The Challenge of Crime in a Free Society* (New York: Dutton, 1968), p. 155. Recidivism, I think, is much more an indicator of police behavior than of criminal behavior. The major method of police investigation is the questioning of "known offenders," not an independent examination of a crime. (See David Matza, *Becoming Deviant* (Englewood Cliffs, N.J.: Prentice-Hall, 1969), p. 196, for an excellent discussion of this problem.) Therefore, it is surprising that even 20 percent of arrestees are newly discovered. I argue that there is a criminal class, which is created and shaped by the criminal justice system.

22. The exact yearly number and percent of crimes by recidivists is given below:

Year	Percent	Number	Year	Percent	Number
1859	31	10	1873	36	61
1860	25	18	1874	42	80
1861	29	43	1875	34	76
1862	32	51	1876	36	66
1863	26	24	1877	41	93
1864	21	23	1878	39	78
1865	40	82	1879	40	80
1866	43	66	1880	46	93
1867	34	55	1881	41	99
1868	42	39	1882	36	87
1869	29	47	1883	38	51
1870	32	52	1884	30	58
1871	51	55	1885	36	45
1872	34	57			

According to John Peter Altgeld, *Our Penal Machinery and Its Victims* (Chicago, 1886), pp. 23-24, 58.5 percent of the prisoners in the Milwaukee House of Correction in 1881 were imprisoned for the first time; 51.9 percent of the prisoners in the Chicago House of Correction in 1882 were recidivists. On the other hand, the Illinois Penitentiary in 1882 contained only 16.2 percent recidivists, but Altgeld claims the usual figure for the penitentiary was about 25 percent. While there is no way to check the accuracy of these figures, they do suggest an interesting situation: misdemeanants and minor offenders were far more likely to be repeaters than were felons. This may simply reflect an aspect of the criminal processing system, rather than criminal behavior, but whatever the reason, apparently recidivism for crimes that were a social threat had not increased to near the modern incidence. Further, if we can rely on Altgeld's data, the "criminal class" of recidivists—people who were in and out of jail—was defined by minor infractions, not serious crime.

5. Paupers in Franklin County

1. See Josephine S. Lowell, *Public Relief and Private Charity* (New York, 1884), passim, and esp. chap. 2 and 3. Lowell quotes with favor a report from the Wisconsin State Board of Charities and Reform: " 'All experience shows that the demand for poor relief does not indicate a large amount of suffering which needs to be relieved but a large amount of laxity or corruption on the part of officers and a large amount of public willingness by able-bodied idlers to be fed at the public expense' " (p. 57). David J. Rothman, *The Discovery of the Asylum: Order and Disorder in the New Republic* (Boston: Little, Brown, 1971), discusses the creation of institutions. See also Robert H. Bremner, *From the Depths: The Discovery of Poverty in the United States* (New York: New York University Press, 1956), pp. 47-50. Blanche D. Coll, *Perspectives in Public Welfare: A History* (Washington: Government Printing Office, 1969), pp. 44-60, discusses the use of outdoor relief as a fund for corruption. The *Seventh Annual Report of the Board of State Charities* of Ohio for 1882 (Columbus, 1883), p. 43, hints that the board felt such usage went on in Ohio: "Needless burdens are imposed upon the public by indiscriminate giving to the poor, or a possible perversion of the fund to other purposes than those contemplated by the law."

2. The time parameters of the poorhouse data are somewhat arbitrary. The remaining records begin in June 1867, thus limiting the earlier end of the time period in an unfortunate manner. My decision to end the data series in December 1881 was dictated by several considerations. First, evidence indicates that the children's home was taking away a segment of the poorhouse population. By 1883 state law required the removal of all children from county infirmaries, but Franklin County had had a home as early as 1877. One hundred and four children were present in the home in September 1881 and 177 were reported as having entered and departed in the previous years by the *Seventh Annual Report of the Board of State Charities* for 1882. Yet apparently the home was not in actual operation in 1878 because the *Third Annual Report* (Columbus, 1879) has no mention of the home. Second, there was a large drop in admissions in 1881. And third, the considerable costs involved in extending the coding and keypunching beyond 1881 did not justify the low information payoff.

An additional limitation to the nature of the poorhouse sample of paupers should be noted here. There were many forms of private charity in Columbus, especially small institutions. A portion of the welfare recipients from these places ended up in the poorhouse, and probably many people from the poorhouse received aid from private institutions. Jacob H. Studer, *Columbus, Ohio: Its History, Resources and Progress* (Columbus, 1873), pp. 227-242, describes the charitable institutions of the city. These included the Columbus Female Benevolent Society (annual budget of $1,797 with an unknown number of clients); the Hannah Neil Mission and Home of the Friendless which housed 167 different individuals in 1871, 25 percent women and 75 percent children; the Women's Home which served 46 "destitute fallen women" in 1870, with a 25 percent restoration rate; Hare Orphans' Home which served about 14 children per year; the Saint Francis Hospital which treated about 500 "sick, aged, infirm, and poor persons" per year; the House of the Good Shepard for Penitent Females had 39 penitents and 48 children in it in 1872. (Ironically, the author of the local history here cited, Jacob Studer, was arrested, although not convicted, for running an illegal lottery in the late 1870s.)

3. Merle Haggard, "If We Make It through December," copyright, Shade Tree Music, BMI (1973).

4. Aileen E. Kennedy, *The Ohio Poor Law and Its Administration* (Chicago: University of Chicago Press, 1934), passim, discusses the rather confusing official attitude toward blacks in the poorhouse. Although not explicitly forbidden from the poorhouse, it seems clear they were not welcome and, one suspects, were victims of de facto discrimination.

5. See apps. 6, 7 and 8 in Monkkonen, "Crime and Poverty in a Nineteenth Century City: The 'Dangerous Class' of Columbus, Ohio, 1860-1885," (Ph.D. diss., University of Minnesota, 1973).

6. Kennedy, p. 45.

7. See, for instance, the column, "The City," in the *Ohio State Journal* (April 15, 1874) for a report of twenty "sleepers" in the cellar of the police station house.

8. See Monkkonen, app. 7, for a complete monthly tabulation.

9. Quoted in Jacob H. Dorn, *Washington Gladden: Prophet of the Social Gospel* (Columbus: Ohio University Press, 1966), p. 310.

6. Paupers

1. John G. Cawelti, *Apostles of the Self-Made Man* (Chicago: University of Chicago Press, 1965), pp. 172-174.

2. Robert L. Dugdale, *The Jukes: A Study in Crime, Pauperism, Disease, and Heredity* (New York: Arno, 1970).

3. This chapter deals only with those paupers found in the 1870 manuscript census or in the city directories issued between 1860 and 1883. Thus in its data base it is comparable to Chapter 4. A total of 174 paupers were positively identified in the census, while an additional 1,124 were identified in the city directories. Unlike the criminals, whose linkage depended only on name matching, the paupers could be more carefully matched by age and place of birth in the census manuscript. However, like the criminals, the city directory matches could be by name only, so the accuracy is not as reliable as is that of the census linkages.

The absolute number of the paupers found in the census was only about one half the total number of criminals found, and the proportion of paupers identified is much lower—only about 8 percent of those giving their residences as within the county, compared to one third for the criminals. Doubles (that is, two or more persons with the same name) add another 2.5 percent, while the city directory identifications add 29 percent for the whole period, or 57 percent of the urban male residents over 20 years old.

4. The possibility should be noted that rural/urban differences are the result of mobility differences, the urban poor being more mobile than the rural, with the result that an overly high proportion of rural poor were found in the census search.

5. For example, 17 persons who entered the poorhouse in 1868 were found in the 1870 census manuscript. These persons represent about 5 percent of the total number of persons claiming local residence entering the poorhouse in 1868. When this figure has been established for the years between 1867 and 1875, the results indicate the presence or absence of persons from the yearly poorhouse cohorts appearing in the census. The results, then, are an aggregate indicator of the disappearance rate of paupers from the city for the years before 1870 and an indicator of the arrival rate of paupers after 1870.

6. See Aileen E. Kennedy, *The Ohio Poor Law and Its Administration* (Chicago: University of Chicago Press, 1934), chaps. 3 and 4, passim, on the "warning out" of paupers in Ohio.

7. Washington Gladden, "The Problem of Poverty," *Century,* 23 (December 1892), p. 250.

8. Because the directory search procedure involved searching for an individual up to three years before or two years after he or she entered the poorhouse, the occupations or jobs might not have been claimed by the person upon entering the poorhouse.

9. Stephan Thernstrom, *Progress and Poverty* (New York: Atheneum, 1970), p. 20.

10. Ohio, Bureau of Labor Statistics, *Third Annual Report, 1879* (Columbus, 1880), p. 219.

11. Thernstrom, pp. 20-22.

12. The table below provides some contemporary data on AFDC families' fathers' occupations and the general U.S. population, which I have tried to make comparable to the nineteenth century data. Overall, it appears that the nineteenth century paupers were located in between the twentieth century welfare recipients and the whole population. Ten percent fewer nineteenth century paupers had no job listed in the directories, but the difference may have been much greater than this, for the probability is that the directories often listed no jobs when the persons could not be contacted. The unskilled category from the 1870 census sample compares closely with the AFDC fathers, and since the census sample included farm laborers who were excluded from the directories, I take the comparison to be reliable. There were fewer AFDC fathers in the semiskilled class than either of the nineteenth century samples, while the AFDC skilled occupational group falls in between the census and directory samples. Both nineteenth century samples are consistently higher than the AFDC sample in the proprietory class, while the AFDC professional group falls between the nineteenth century samples.

Occupations of AFDC fathers and the

general population, 1960 (in percent)

	No job (unknown)	Un-skilled	Semi-skilled	Skilled	Propri-etor	Profes-sional
AFDC	25.1	43.9	5.6	22.8	2.0	0.6
General population	4.6	9.7	6.1	53.6	16.2	10.3

Source: David Matza, "Poverty and Disrepute," in Robert K. Merton and Robert A. Nisbet, eds., *Contemporary Social Problems* (New York: Harcourt, Brace and World, 1966), p. 631.

13. Mary R. Smith, "Almshouse Women," *American Statistical Association Publications*, 6 (1895), 225, table 1, provides recidivism data for the San Francisco Almshouse. Her data indicates that over the period 1889-94, 64.6 percent of the almshouse inmates were admitted for the first time. Taken by year there is no consistent trend. Unfortunately, there is no indication as to whether or not this includes admittances to other almshouses; however, her individually interviewed inmates reported a 63 percent first time admittance rate. If the rates for the whole almshouse are self-reported, then they cover more than just one place. We might infer, then, that there was an approximate 35 percent return rate to any institution, which compares to the 14 percent rate for the Franklin County Infirmary alone.

14. Eric J. Hobsbawm and George Rude, *Captain Swing* (London: Lawrence, 1969), p. 35.

15. Michael Harrington, *The Other America: Poverty in the United States* (Baltimore: Macmillan, 1962), p. 17.

16. Jacob Henry Dorn, *Washington Gladden: Prophet of the Social Gospel* (Columbus: Ohio State University Press, 1966), p. 278.

7. *The Dangerous Class*

1. By estimating the total population moving through Franklin County and using the known number of criminals and paupers, the random chance of a criminal also being a pauper is calculated to have been 17.6 per thousand criminals. By chance alone there should have been 39 criminal/paupers between 1867 and 1881. Instead, there were 157 or 4.02 times as many as accidentally possible. By this rather severe measure, 118 persons, or 5.38 percent of the criminals, were driven to crime by their socioeconomic condition.

More precisely, the method of estimating the chances of a criminal also being a pauper is given by the formula:

$$E = \frac{P_I}{[(Y \times M_r)\,(P_f)] + P_{nI}}$$

where E is the ratio of criminal/paupers per one thousand criminals, Y is the number of years being examined, M_r is the mobility ratio (.4. See Peter Knights, *The Plain People of Boston* [New York: Oxford University Press, 1971], p. 62.), P_f is the mean population of Franklin County in the period being examined, P_{nI} is the population of the poorhouse nonresidents, and P_I is the total poorhouse population.

2. Robert L. Dugdale, *The Jukes: A Study in Crime, Pauperism, Disease, and Heredity* (New York: Arno, 1970), p. 47, sets up a continuum from the "ideal pauper" to the "ideal criminal." The pauper, he says, is "unable to help himself," while the criminal is a "courageous man" of action.

3. Eugene J. Webb, Donald T. Campbell, Richard D. Schwartz, and Lee Sechrest, *Unobtrusive Measures: Nonreactive Research in the Social Sciences* (Chicago: Rand McNally, 1966).

4. One recent exception is Michael Lesy, *Wisconsin Death Trip* (New York: Pantheon, 1973).

5. Josiah Flynt [Willard], *Tramping with Tramps: Studies and Sketches of Vagabond Life* (New York, 1899). The one recent study of nineteenth century tramps, Paul T. Ringenbach's *Tramps and Reformers, 1873-1916: The Discovery of Unemployment in New York* (Westport: Greenwood, 1973), although it adds nothing new about the tramps themselves, corrects Flynt's elitist attitude and includes a good discussion of the social attitude toward tramps.

6. John J. McCook, "A Tramp Census and Its Revelations," *Forum* (August 1893), pp. 753-766, presents data on tramps from a survey he made in 1892. Sixty percent of his tramps were under 35, 8.5 percent had poor health, and 56 percent were native born.

7. Lida Rose McCabe, *Don't You Remember?* (Columbus, 1884). See, "The Doctor's Story," pp. 242-294, for the full account of the matchgirl from Todd Barracks and the tramp who turned out to be an earl.

Index

183

Index